SIMPLY STYLISH PERFECT PASTA

CAROLYN HUMPHRIES

foulsham
LONDON • NEW YORK • TORONTO • SYDNEY

foulsham
The Publishing House, Bennetts Close,
Cippenham, Slough, Berkshire, SL1 5AP, England

ISBN 0-572-02466-5

Printed in Great Britain by Cox & Wyman Ltd, Reading

CONTENTS

Introduction	4
All About Pasta	5
Storecupboard Standbys	7
Notes on the Recipes	10
Accompaniments	11
Meat and Poultry Dishes	13
Seafood Dishes	49
Vegetable Dishes	78
Cheese, Egg and Cream Dishes	117
Salads	136
Oils, Butters and Pastes	145
Index	158

INTRODUCTION

Did you know that there are over 600 different pasta shapes produced in Italy? Many of them are now available in supermarkets everywhere. Fresh and dried, there is a whole range of delectable flavours and colours too – the standard pale, creamy durum wheat; the more golden, egg pasta; the popular green, spinach; the rustic wholewheat; the glorious orangey, sun-dried tomato; the black, mushroom or squid ink and the speckled olive- or herb-flavoured to name just a few. Strands or tubes, pretty shapes or delicately stuffed little parcels, pasta is one of the most popular and versatile staple foods today. It can be bathed in sumptuous sauces, tossed in flavoured oils or butters or layered and baked to perfection. In this book you'll find versions of all the famous Italian dishes plus a veritable mountain of my own mouthwatering ideas specially created for pasta lovers everywhere.

ALL ABOUT PASTA

Pasta Varieties

It is impossible to list every shape and strand in this little book, but here are some of those you are most likely to use. Most varieties are available fresh or dried.

Strands
Long threads of pasta in different thicknesses.

- *Spaghetti:* probably the best known of all pastas, it is long, thin and straight
- *Capelli d'angelo* or *Capellini:* 'angel hair', the thinnest of all
- *Fusilli:* 'fuses' – thick twisted spaghetti
- *Spaghettini:* 'little spaghetti'
- *Vermicelli:* 'little worms'

Tubes
There are many shapes and sizes of tubes. These are some of the most common.

- *Bucatini:* long macaroni, like spaghetti but thicker with a hole in the middle
- *Cannelloni:* large fat tubes, serve stuffed
- *Ditali:* short-cut macaroni, narrow tubes
- *Elbow macaroni:* short, curved, narrow tubes
- *Penne:* quill-shaped tubes
- *Rigatoni:* ribbed tubes
- *Zite:* wide macaroni cut in short lengths

Shapes
There is a superb variety of shapes to choose from, including the following types.

- *Conchiglie:* conch-shaped shells
- *Farfalle:* butterflies
- *Lumachi:* snail-shaped shells
- *Maltagliate:* 'badly cut' pasta. Make from fresh pasta (see page 156)
- *Maruzze:* shells of varying sizes
- *Rotelli* or *twistetti:* spirals
- *Ruote:* wheels

Ribbon Noodles
These are made from flat pasta cut into varying widths, sometimes kept flat, sometimes with a rippled edge.

- *Fettuccine:* flat ribbons about 5 mm/¼ in wide
- *Fettuccelli:* narrow fettuccine
- *Fettucci:* as above, but about 1 cm/½ in wide
- *Linguini:* very narrow ribbons, like flattened spaghetti
- *Mafalde:* wide ribbons with a rippled edge
- *Pappardelle:* wide ribbons about 2 cm/¾ in wide
- *Tagliarini:* narrow tagliatelle (see below)
- *Tagliatelle:* similar to fettuccine

Stuffed Shapes
Cheese, spinach, mushroom and meat stuffings are all popular.

- *Agnolotti:* small, filled half-moons
- *Cappelletti:* little, filled hat shapes
- *Ravioli:* stuffed cushions
- *Tortellini:* small crescent shapes joined into rings

STORECUPBOARD STANDBYS

If you keep most of these in your kitchen, you will be able to knock up a sensational pasta meal in a moment. These are not all the ingredients used in this book, but they form the basis of many delicious dishes. As you discover new recipes you like, add those ingredients to your store.

Taste Ticklers

- Tube of tomato purée (paste)
- Jar of passata (sieved tomatoes)
- Dried herbs: mixed or oregano are essential plus, preferably, mint, basil, rosemary, thyme and bay leaves, bouquet garni sachets and dill (dill weed)
- Fresh corm of garlic, or a tube of purée, or dried granules/powder
- Whole black peppercorns and a mill, or coarsely ground black pepper
- Salt
- Mustard – Dijon essential, plus, preferably, English and grainy
- Vinegar – red wine, white wine or cider (no need for malt too unless you prefer it)
- Stock cubes – vegetable essential, plus, preferably, chicken and beef
- Spices – nutmeg, cinnamon, paprika and chilli or cayenne
- Curry paste or powder
- Redcurrant jelly (clear conserve)
- Olive oil essential, plus, preferably, sunflower and walnut oil
- Olives in jars or cans
- Pickled capers
- Sugar – caster (superfine) essential, plus light brown preferably
- Clear honey
- Dried milk (non-fat dry milk)
- UHT whipping cream
- Lemon juice
- Booze – red and white wine, sherry, brandy

Clever Cans and Packets

- Tomatoes
- Tuna
- Sweetcorn (corn)
- Cannellini and red kidney beans
- Chick peas (garbanzos)
- Pimientos
- Condensed soups
- Sauces – white and cheese
- Nuts – flaked (slivered) almonds, walnut halves, chopped mixed nuts

Fridge and Freezer Friends

- Medium eggs
- Cheeses – Parmesan and Cheddar essential, Mozzarella and a blue cheese preferable
- Unsalted butter
- Sunflower or olive oil spread (suitable for cooking as well as spreading)
- Good quality mayonnaise (I use a 'light' variety)
- Frozen peas
- Frozen prawns (shrimp)
- Frozen herbs – parsley, coriander (cilantro) and basil are good

Essentials

- Pasta shapes and strands (I usually keep spaghetti, lasagne, tagliatelle, short-cut macaroni and rigatoni or penne and buy others as I feel like them)
- Plain (all-purpose) flour
- Cornflour (cornstarch)
- Part-baked ciabatta and/or French sticks

NOTES ON THE RECIPES

- Use either fresh or dried pasta for any of the recipes. In my opinion, fresh is best but dried is more economical and still makes memorable eating.
- When following a recipe, use either metric, imperial or American measures, never mix them up.
- All spoon measures are level: 15 ml = 1 tbsp
5 ml = 1 tsp
- All eggs are medium unless otherwise stated.
- When using fresh produce, always wash, dry, peel and core or remove seeds as necessary.
- All preparation and cooking times are approximate and should be used as a guide only.
- Fresh herbs are used unless dried are specifically called for. If substituting dried, use half the quantity or less as they are very pungent. There is no substitute for fresh parsley, basil or coriander. Use frozen rather than dried, if possible.
- Every recipe calls for a specific type of pasta but you can use different shapes or strands as you like.
- The recipes call for specific quantities of pasta. You can increase or decrease the amount according to appetites – you'll just have more or less sauce!
- Many pasta sauces do not contain meat or fish so are suitable for vegetarians. Make sure any cheese you use is also suitable.
- Tubs of Parmesan are all right for everyday use but the flavour does not match that of fresh. It is tiresome to grate every time you use it, however, so I suggest you grate a large piece (ideally using a food processor for speed) and freeze it in a container. You can spoon out just what you need when you need it. I also suggest shaving another piece with a potato peeler and freezing the shavings in a separate container.

ACCOMPANIMENTS

The lovely thing about pasta is it needs very little accompaniment. However, as the sauces can be quite rich, a simple salad and/or some warm crusty bread will round off the meal to perfection.

Simple Salads

Crisp Leaf Salad

Either buy a bag of ready-prepared mixed leaves from your supermarket (expensive but useful if you're short of time) or make your own selection from the numerous varieties available. Tear rather than chop and place in a bowl. Dress with a simple vinaigrette: 3 parts olive oil to 1 part wine vinegar. Season with salt, pepper and a pinch of caster (superfine) sugar.

Tomato and Onion Salad

Slice firm, ripe tomatoes and place in a shallow dish. Top with thinly sliced onion rings and dress with vinaigrette (see above). Sprinkle with chopped parsley or a few torn basil leaves and leave to stand for 30 minutes to allow the flavours to develop.

Mixed Green Salad

Mix any types of green salad leaves in a bowl. Add sliced cucumber, green (bell) pepper, cut into thin strips or rings, a few chopped spring onions (scallions) and sliced avocado, dipped in lemon juice. Add a little Dijon mustard to the vinaigrette (see above) and sprinkle the whole thing with salad cress.

Beautiful Breads

A warm ordinary crusty loaf is delicious but you could try something a little more adventurous. The best speciality breads to go with pasta are focaccia, ciabatta (plain or flavoured with olives, mushrooms, sun-dried tomatoes, herbs, garlic or walnuts) or French bread, either plain or one of the ready-to-bake flavoured-butter baguettes like garlic, herb, cheese, or cheese and bacon.

MEAT & POULTRY DISHES

Pasta is a wonderful way of making a little meat go a long way. It is the perfect vehicle for every type of meat from lamb to beef, pork to bacon and every kind of poultry too. From the classics like Cannelloni Ripieni and Spaghetti with Meatballs to my favourites, Cured Ham and Pea Shells and Macaroni with Smoked Pork Sausage and Greens, you'll find a whole range of substantial and delicious meaty main meals.

Family Spaghetti Bolognese

This is a quick everyday favourite of mine, but not an authentic Italian recipe. See page 16 for Tagliatelle Bolognese Classico.

SERVES 4	METRIC	IMPERIAL	AMERICAN
Minced (ground) beef or lamb	*350 g*	*12 oz*	*3 cups*
Onion, chopped	*1*	*1*	*1*
Garlic clove, crushed	*1*	*1*	*1*
Can of chopped tomatoes	*400 g*	*14 oz*	*1 large*
Tomato purée (paste)	*15 ml*	*1 tbsp*	*1 tbsp*
Salt and freshly ground black pepper			
Dried oregano	*5 ml*	*1 tsp*	*1 tsp*
Pinch of caster (superfine) sugar	*1*	*1*	*1*
Spaghetti	*350 g*	*12 oz*	*12 oz*
Freshly grated Parmesan cheese, to garnish			

1 Put the meat, onion and garlic in a saucepan. Cook, stirring, until the meat is well browned and the grains are separate.

2 Add the remaining ingredients. Stir well. Bring to the boil, reduce the heat, half-cover and simmer gently for 15–20 minutes until a rich sauce has formed. Stir gently from time to time.

3 Meanwhile, cook the spaghetti according to the packet directions. Drain. Pile on to warm plates, spoon the Bolognese sauce over and sprinkle with Parmesan cheese before serving.

PREPARATION TIME: 5 MINUTES

COOKING TIME: 15–20 MINUTES

For a Simple Meat Lasagne

Make the Bolognese sauce (left). Spread a spoonful of the meat mixture in the base of a fairly shallow ovenproof dish. Top with sheets of no-need-to-precook lasagne. Add half the remaining sauce, more lasagne, the rest of the sauce and then a final layer of lasagne. Top with cheese sauce (see Macaroni Cheese page 118) and cook in the oven at 190°C/375°F/gas mark 5 for 35 minutes until cooked through and golden brown. Alternatively, microwave for 10–15 minutes or until the lasagne feels tender when a knife is inserted down through the centre. Then place under a hot grill (broiler) to brown the top.

Tagliatelle Bolognese Classico

Italian housewives would simmer this sauce for several hours, moistening with a little more wine as necessary. Try doing so yourself, if you have the time. For an even better flavour, leave it to stand overnight and then reheat it the following day.

SERVES 6	METRIC	IMPERIAL	AMERICAN
Olive oil	*45 ml*	*3 tbsp*	*3 tbsp*
Onions, finely chopped	*2*	*2*	*2*
Garlic cloves, crushed	*2*	*2*	*2*
Carrot, finely chopped	*1*	*1*	*1*
Celery stick, finely chopped	*1*	*1*	*1*
Minced (ground) beef	*450 g*	*1 lb*	*4 cups*
Streaky bacon rashers (slices), chopped	*3*	*3*	*3*
Ripe beefsteak tomatoes, skinned, seeded and chopped	*3*	*3*	*3*
OR can of chopped tomatoes	*400 g*	*14 oz*	*1 large*
Beef stock	*150 ml*	*¼ pt*	*⅔ cup*
Wineglass of red wine	*1*	*1*	*1*
Thick slice of lemon	*1*	*1*	*1*
Bay leaf	*1*	*1*	*1*
Salt and freshly ground black pepper			
Tomato purée (paste)	*15 ml*	*1 tbsp*	*1 tbsp*
Double (heavy) cream (optional)	*30 ml*	*2 tbsp*	*2 tbsp*
Tagliatelle	*450 g*	*1 lb*	*1 lb*
Freshly grated Parmesan cheese, to garnish			

1 Heat the olive oil in a large saucepan and fry (sauté) the onion, garlic, carrot and celery for 3 minutes until softened but not browned.

2 Add the beef and bacon and fry, stirring, until browned and the grains of meat are separate.

3 Add the tomatoes, stock, wine, the thick slice of lemon and the bay leaf. Season with salt and pepper and bring to the boil, stirring.

4 Reduce the heat and simmer gently, uncovered, for about 30 minutes, until the sauce is well reduced and thick (or cook in a slo-cooker for 5–6 hours).

5 Discard the lemon slice and bay leaf. Taste and re-season, if necessary. Stir in the cream, if using.

6 Cook the tagliatelle according to the packet directions. Drain and pile on to plates. Spoon the Bolognese sauce over and sprinkle with Parmesan cheese before serving.

PREPARATION TIME:
10 MINUTES

COOKING TIME:
38 MINUTES

Lasagne Al Forno

SERVES 6

Make the Bolognese Classico Sauce (left). Layer with sheets of no-need-to-precook lasagne in a large shallow ovenproof dish, finishing with lasagne sheets. Top with a Parmesan cheese sauce (see Mushroom Lasagne page 96) and sprinkle with grated Parmesan. Cook in a preheated oven at 190°C/375°F/gas mark 5 for 40 minutes.

Bucatini with Steak Sauce

This is a quick version of a sauce my gran used to call 'Bolognese' when I was a child. It's nothing like the Italian sauce, but it is truly delicious. She would prepare it in a flameproof casserole, then cook in the oven at 160°C/325°F/gas mark 3 for about 3 hours (which is worth doing, if you have the time).

SERVES 4–6	METRIC	IMPERIAL	AMERICAN
Onions, finely chopped	*2*	*2*	*2*
Dripping or lard (shortening)	*25 g*	*1 oz*	*2 tbsp*
Lean top rump steak, minced (ground)	*450 g*	*1 lb*	*4 cups*
Beef stock	*450 ml*	*¾ pt*	*2 cups*
A little gravy block or browning			
Salt and freshly ground black pepper			
Plain (all-purpose) flour	*20 g*	*¾ oz*	*3 tbsp*
Bucatini	*350 g*	*12 oz*	*12 oz*
Warmed passata (sieved tomatoes) or tomato ketchup (catsup) and chopped parsley, to garnish			

1 Fry (sauté) the onion in the dripping until softened and lightly golden.

2 Add the steak and fry, stirring, until browned and the grains are separate.

3 Add the stock and a little gravy block or browning. Half-cover and simmer gently for 30–40 minutes until really tender (or cook in a pressure cooker for 20 minutes or a slo-cooker for up to 6 hours).

4 Blend the flour with a little water until smooth. Stir into the meat and bring to the boil. Simmer, stirring, for 2 minutes. Season to taste with salt and pepper.

5 Meanwhile, cook the bucatini according to the packet directions. Drain. Pile on to warm plates. Top with the meat sauce and drizzle with a little warmed passata or tomato ketchup and sprinkle with chopped parsley.

PREPARATION TIME: 5 MINUTES

COOKING TIME: 45 MINUTES

Beef Stroganoff

This special-occasion sauce is ideal for a dinner party and makes a little fillet steak go a long way.

SERVES 4	METRIC	IMPERIAL	AMERICAN
Fillet steak	*225 g*	*8 oz*	*8 oz*
Butter	*50 g*	*2 oz*	*¼ cup*
Onions, thinly sliced	*2*	*2*	*2*
Button mushrooms, sliced	*100 g*	*4 oz*	*4 oz*
Salt and freshly ground black pepper			
Brandy	*15 ml*	*1 tbsp*	*1 tbsp*
Soured (dairy sour) cream	*150 ml*	*¼ pt*	*⅔ cup*
Tagliatelle	*225 g*	*8 oz*	*8 oz*
A knob of butter and chopped parsley, to garnish			

1 Cut the steak into thin strips about 2.5 cm/1 in long.

2 Heat half the butter in a large frying pan (skillet). Add the onions and fry (sauté) for 2–3 minutes until softened and lightly golden.

3 Add the mushrooms and continue cooking, stirring, for 2–3 minutes until cooked through. Remove from the pan and reserve.

4 Heat the remaining butter and add the beef. Season well with salt and pepper and fry, stirring, for about 3 minutes until just cooked through.

5 Add the brandy, ignite and shake the pan until the flames subside.

6 Return the onions and mushrooms to the pan with any cooking juices. Stir in the cream and heat through.

7 Meanwhile, break the tagliatelle into small pieces and cook according to the packet directions. Drain and toss in the knob of butter.

8 Spoon to one side of warm serving plates. Spoon the Stroganoff mixture beside and sprinkle with chopped parsley.

PREPARATION TIME: 10 MINUTES

COOKING TIME: 10 MINUTES

Spaghetti with Meatballs

For a plainer version, omit the chilli, coriander and cumin and add 5 ml/1 tsp dried oregano to the meat mixture instead.

SERVES 4	METRIC	IMPERIAL	AMERICAN
Minced (ground) lamb or beef	*450 g*	*1 lb*	*4 cups*
Onion, finely chopped	*1*	*1*	*1*
Garlic clove, crushed (optional)	*1*	*1*	*1*
Fresh breadcrumbs	*50 g*	*2 oz*	*1 cup*
Chilli powder	*1.5 ml*	*¼ tsp*	*¼ tsp*
Ground coriander (cilantro)	*1.5 ml*	*¼ tsp*	*¼ tsp*
Ground cumin	*1.5 ml*	*¼ tsp*	*¼ tsp*
Salt and freshly ground black pepper			
Egg	*1*	*1*	*1*
Oil for frying			
Jar of passata (sieved tomatoes)	*550 g*	*1¼ lb*	*1 large*
Dried oregano	*5 ml*	*1 tsp*	*1 tsp*
Spaghetti	*350 g*	*12 oz*	*12 oz*
Freshly grated Parmesan cheese, to serve			

1 Mix the meat, onion, garlic, breadcrumbs, spices and a little salt and pepper thoroughly in a bowl.

2 Add the beaten egg and mix well to bind. Shape into small balls.

3 Fry (sauté) in hot oil for about 3 minutes until golden brown. Drain on kitchen paper.

4 Pour the passata into a saucepan. Add the oregano and meatballs. Simmer for 10 minutes, stirring gently occasionally.

5 Meanwhile, cook the spaghetti according to the packet directions. Drain.

6 Pile the spaghetti on warm plates. Spoon over the meatballs and sauce and top with grated Parmesan cheese.

PREPARATION TIME:
15 MINUTES

COOKING TIME:
13 MINUTES

Cannelloni Ripieni

SERVES 4	METRIC	IMPERIAL	AMERICAN
Sauce:			
Onion, finely chopped	*1*	*1*	*1*
Tomatoes, skinned and chopped	*900 g*	*2 lb*	*2 lb*
Dried oregano	*2.5 ml*	*½ tsp*	*½ tsp*
Dried thyme	*2.5 ml*	*½ tsp*	*½ tsp*
Salt and freshly ground black pepper			
Filling:			
Pancetta, finely minced (ground)	*225 g*	*8 oz*	*2 cups*
Chopped parsley	*15 ml*	*1 tbsp*	*1 tbsp*
Garlic cloves, crushed	*2*	*2*	*2*
Egg, beaten	*1*	*1*	*1*
No-need-to-precook cannelloni tubes	*8–12*	*8–12*	*8–12*
Parmesan cheese, freshly grated	*100 g*	*4 oz*	*1 cup*

1 Make the sauce. Heat 15 ml/1 tbsp of the oil in a pan. Add the onion and fry (sauté) gently for 3 minutes until softened but not browned.

2 Add the chopped tomatoes and herbs, season and simmer for 20 minutes, stirring occasionally.

3 Make the filling. Heat 30 ml/2 tbsp of the remaining oil. Add the pancetta, parsley and garlic. Fry for 3 minutes, stirring. Turn into a bowl and cool.

4 Beat in the egg and then, using a small spoon, fill the cannelloni tubes with this mixture.

5 Lay the filled tubes in an oiled ovenproof dish. Pour the tomato sauce over.

6 Sprinkle with the cheese and cook in a preheated oven at 190°C/375°F/gas mark 5 for about 35 minutes until cooked through and bubbling.

PREPARATION TIME: 10 MINUTES

COOKING TIME: 58 MINUTES

Pasta all'Amatriciana

SERVES 4	METRIC	IMPERIAL	AMERICAN
Bucatini	*350 g*	*12 oz*	*12 oz*
Salt			
Streaky bacon rashers (slices), rinded	*8*	*8*	*8*
Olive oil	*15 ml*	*1 tbsp*	*1 tbsp*
Small onion, finely chopped	*1*	*1*	*1*
Freshly grated Parmesan cheese	*60 ml*	*4 tbsp*	*4 tbsp*
A few torn basil leaves, to garnish			

1 Cook the bucatini according to the packet directions. Drain and return to the pan.

2 Meanwhile, dry-fry (sauté) the bacon until crisp. Remove from the frying pan (skillet), crumble into pieces and reserve.

3 Add the oil to the frying pan and, when hot, add the onion. Fry, stirring, for 5 minutes until soft and golden. Add the bacon and cheese and stir well.

4 Pour over the bucatini and toss well. Pile into warm bowls and sprinkle with a few torn basil leaves.

PREPARATION TIME: 5 MINUTES

COOKING TIME: 12 MINUTES

Mozzarella-topped Veal and Pork Rigatoni

SERVES 4	METRIC	IMPERIAL	AMERICAN
Minced (ground) veal	*175 g*	*6 oz*	*1½ cups*
Minced (ground) pork	*175 g*	*6 oz*	*1½ cups*
Onion, finely chopped	*1*	*1*	*1*
Garlic cloves, crushed	*2*	*2*	*2*
Olive oil	*15 ml*	*1 tbsp*	*1 tbsp*
White wine	*150 ml*	*¼ pt*	*⅔ cup*
Can of chopped tomatoes	*400 g*	*14 oz*	*1 large*
Dried thyme	*2.5 ml*	*½ tsp*	*½ tsp*
Salt and freshly ground black pepper			
Rigatoni	*225 g*	*8 oz*	*8 oz*
To serve:			
Grated Mozzarella cheese	*60 ml*	*4 tbsp*	*4 tbsp*
Freshly grated Parmesan cheese	*30 ml*	*2 tbsp*	*2 tbsp*

1 Fry (sauté) the meats, onion and garlic in the oil, stirring until browned and all meat grains are separate.

2 Add the wine, tomatoes, thyme and seasoning.

3 Bring to the boil, reduce the heat, part-cover and simmer until nearly all the liquid has evaporated and the sauce is thick. Taste and re-season, if necessary.

4 Cook the rigatoni according to the packet directions. Drain, toss with the sauce and spoon on to flame-proof plates. Sprinkle with the cheeses and flash under a hot grill (broiler) to melt.

PREPARATION TIME:
5 MINUTES

COOKING TIME:
35 MINUTES

Parma Ham and Mushroom Penne

Any raw thin-sliced ham can be used in this recipe.

SERVES 4	METRIC	IMPERIAL	AMERICAN
Penne	*225 g*	*8 oz*	*8 oz*
Olive oil	*30 ml*	*2 tbsp*	*2 tbsp*
Button mushrooms, sliced	*100 g*	*4 oz*	*4 oz*
Yeast extract	*5 ml*	*1 tsp*	*1 tsp*
Parma ham, cut into thin strips	*100 g*	*4 oz*	*4 oz*
Butter	*25 g*	*1 oz*	*2 tbsp*
Crème fraîche	*75 ml*	*5 tbsp*	*5 tbsp*
Salt and freshly ground black pepper			
Grated nutmeg	*1.5 ml*	*¼ tsp*	*¼ tsp*
Freshly grated Parmesan or Pecorino cheese, to serve			

1 Cook the penne according to the packet directions.

2 Heat the oil in a small saucepan and add the mushrooms. Cook gently for 2 minutes until soft.

3 Stir in the yeast extract, ham and the butter in small flakes. Heat gently, stirring, until the butter melts.

4 Stir in the crème fraîche, salt and pepper to taste and the nutmeg. Heat through for 2 minutes.

5 Add to the cooked penne and toss well over a gentle heat before serving with freshly grated Parmesan or Pecorino cheese.

PREPARATION TIME:
5 MINUTES

COOKING TIME:
10–15 MINUTES

Macaroni with Smoked Pork Sausage and Greens

Ring the changes with chorizo or other spiced sausage.

SERVES 4	METRIC	IMPERIAL	AMERICAN
Macaroni	*225 g*	*8 oz*	*8 oz*
Olive oil	*90 ml*	*6 tbsp*	*6 tbsp*
Leeks, sliced	*2*	*2*	*2*
Garlic cloves, crushed	*2*	*2*	*2*
Spring greens (spring cabbage), shredded	*350 g*	*12 oz*	*12 oz*
Smoked pork ring, sliced	*1*	*1*	*1*
Water	*45 ml*	*3 tbsp*	*3 tbsp*
Salt and freshly ground black pepper			
Stoned (pitted) black olives, sliced	*8*	*8*	*8*
Butter	*15 g*	*½ oz*	*1 tbsp*
Cayenne, to garnish			
Freshly grated Gouda cheese, to serve			

1 Cook the macaroni according to the packet directions. Drain.

2 Meanwhile, heat 60 ml/4 tbsp of the oil in a large saucepan. Add the leeks and garlic, cover and cook gently for 5 minutes until softened but not browned.

3 Add the greens and cook, stirring, for a few minutes until they begin to 'fall'. Add the sliced sausage and the water. Cover and cook gently for 5 minutes or until soft, stirring occasionally.

4 Add the remaining oil and the olives and butter and season with a little salt and plenty of pepper.

5 Add the cooked macaroni, toss well and serve in bowls sprinkled with cayenne and a little grated Gouda cheese.

PREPARATION TIME: 10 MINUTES

COOKING TIME: 20 MINUTES

Cured Ham and Pea Shells

SERVES 4	METRIC	IMPERIAL	AMERICAN
Multi-coloured conchiglie	*225 g*	*8 oz*	*8 oz*
Cooked ham pieces	*225 g*	*8 oz*	*8 oz*
Onions, finely chopped	*2*	*2*	*2*
Unsalted (sweet) butter	*100 g*	*4 oz*	*½ cup*
Olive oil	*15 ml*	*1 tbsp*	*1 tbsp*
Frozen peas	*100 g*	*4 oz*	*4 oz*
Dried mint	*2.5 ml*	*½ tsp*	*½ tsp*
Freshly grated Parmesan cheese	*50 g*	*2 oz*	*½ cup*
Salt and freshly ground black pepper			
A little olive oil, to garnish			
Extra freshly grated Parmesan cheese, to serve			

1 Cook the conchiglie according to the packet directions. Drain.

2 Meanwhile, cut the ham into very small dice, discarding any fat.

3 Fry (sauté) the onion gently in half the butter and the oil until softened but not browned.

4 Add the ham, peas and mint, cover, reduce the heat and cook gently for 5 minutes, stirring occasionally.

5 Add the remaining butter, the cheese, a very little salt and lots of pepper.

6 Toss the cooked conchiglie with the sauce. Drizzle with a little olive oil and serve with Parmesan.

PREPARATION TIME: 5 MINUTES

COOKING TIME: 15 MINUTES

Spaghetti Napoletana

SERVES 4	METRIC	IMPERIAL	AMERICAN
Onion, chopped	*1*	*1*	*1*
Garlic clove, crushed	*1*	*1*	*1*
Olive oil	*30 ml*	*2 tbsp*	*2 tbsp*
Streaky bacon rashers (slices), rinded and diced	*8*	*8*	*8*
Can of chopped tomatoes	*400 g*	*14 oz*	*1 large*
Dried thyme	*5 ml*	*1 tsp*	*1 tsp*
Tomato purée (paste)	*15 ml*	*1 tbsp*	*1 tbsp*
Caster (superfine) sugar	*1.5 ml*	*¼ tsp*	*¼ tsp*
Salt and freshly ground black pepper			
Wholewheat spaghetti	*350 g*	*12 oz*	*12 oz*
Grated Provolone or Cheddar cheese, to serve			

1 Fry (sauté) the onion and garlic in half the oil until softened but not browned. Add the diced bacon and fry, stirring, for 2 minutes.

2 Add the remaining ingredients, except the pasta, bring to the boil, then simmer gently for about 10 minutes until pulpy.

3 Cook the spaghetti according to the packet directions. Drain and toss in the remaining oil.

4 Pile the spaghetti on to warm plates. Top with the bacon and tomato sauce and lots of grated cheese.

PREPARATION TIME:
10 MINUTES

COOKING TIME:
15 MINUTES

Italian Supper

If you don't like spicy food, omit the red chilli from the recipe.

SERVES 4	METRIC	IMPERIAL	AMERICAN
Red onions, sliced	*2*	*2*	*2*
Red (bell) pepper, cut into thin strips	*1*	*1*	*1*
Red chilli, seeded and thinly sliced	*1*	*1*	*1*
Garlic clove, crushed	*1*	*1*	*1*
Olive oil	*45 ml*	*3 tbsp*	*3 tbsp*
Can of chopped tomatoes	*400 g*	*14 oz*	*1 large*
Tomato purée (paste)	*15 ml*	*1 tbsp*	*1 tbsp*
Water	*45 ml*	*3 tbsp*	*3 tbsp*
Dried oregano	*5 ml*	*1 tsp*	*1 tsp*
Stuffed green olives, sliced	*8*	*8*	*8*
Mortadella sausage, diced	*50 g*	*2 oz*	*2 oz*
Milano salami, diced	*50 g*	*2 oz*	*2 oz*
Salt and freshly ground black pepper			
Spaghetti	*350 g*	*12 oz*	*12 oz*
Freshly grated Parmesan or Pecorino cheese, to serve			

1 Fry (sauté) the onion, pepper, chilli and garlic in the oil for 3 minutes until softened but not browned.

2 Add the tomatoes, the tomato purée blended with the water and the oregano. Bring to the boil, reduce the heat and simmer gently for about 10 minutes until pulpy.

3 Add the olives, and the diced sausage and cook for a further 2 minutes. Season to taste with salt, if necessary, and plenty of black pepper.

4 Meanwhile, cook the spaghetti according to the packet directions. Drain.

5 Pile on to warm plates. Top with the sauce and sprinkle with grated Parmesan or Pecorino cheese before serving.

PREPARATION TIME: 10 MINUTES

COOKING TIME: 15 MINUTES

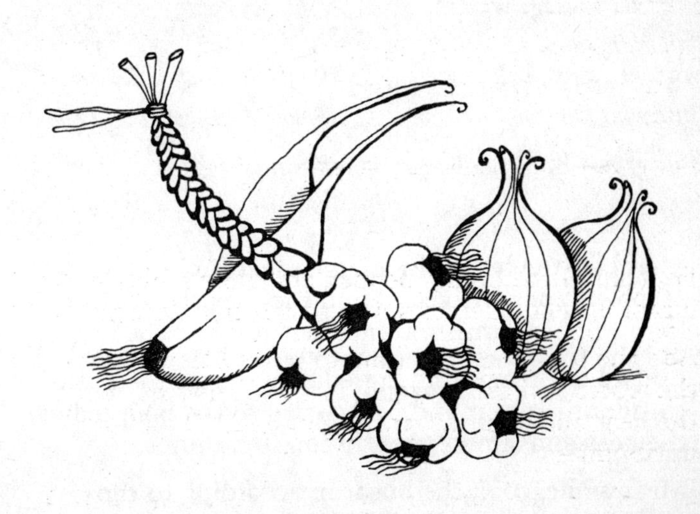

Tangy Ham, Raisin and Pine Nut Bucatini

The salty flavour of the Feta cheese offsets the richness of the sauce in this unusual dish.

SERVES 4	METRIC	IMPERIAL	AMERICAN
Unsalted (sweet) butter	*50 g*	*2 oz*	*¼ cup*
Onion, chopped	*1*	*1*	*1*
Small green (bell) pepper, diced	*1*	*1*	*1*
Celery sticks, diced	*2*	*2*	*2*
Carrot, diced	*1*	*1*	*1*
Raisins	*40 g*	*1½ oz*	*¼ cup*
Tomato purée (paste)	*30 ml*	*2 tbsp*	*2 tbsp*
Ham or chicken stock	*300 ml*	*½ pt*	*1¼ cups*
Cooked ham, diced	*175 g*	*6 oz*	*1½ cups*
Pine nuts	*25 g*	*1 oz*	*¼ cup*
Bucatini	*350 g*	*12 oz*	*12 oz*
Cornflour (cornstarch)	*10 ml*	*2 tsp*	*2 tsp*
White wine vinegar	*15 ml*	*1 tbsp*	*1 tbsp*
Feta cheese, crumbled	*50 g*	*2 oz*	*½ cup*

1 Melt half the butter in a large saucepan. Add the onion, pepper and celery and cook gently, stirring, for 5 minutes until softened but not browned.

2 Add all the remaining ingredients except the pasta, cornflour, vinegar and Feta. Bring to the boil, reduce the heat and simmer gently for 20 minutes.

3 Meanwhile, cook the bucatini according to the packet directions. Drain and toss in the remaining butter.

4 Blend the cornflour with the vinegar. Stir into the sauce and cook until thickened and clear.

5 Pile the pasta on to warm plates. Top with the sauce and scatter the crumbled Feta cheese over.

PREPARATION TIME: 10 MINUTES

COOKING TIME: 26 MINUTES

TV Supper

SERVES 4	METRIC	IMPERIAL	AMERICAN
Macaroni	*225 g*	*8 oz*	*8 oz*
Streaky bacon rashers (slices), diced	*4*	*4*	*4*
Red Leicester cheese, grated	*100 g*	*4 oz*	*1 cup*
Worcestershire sauce	*5 ml*	*1 tsp*	*1 tsp*
Salt and freshly ground black pepper			
Butter	*25 g*	*1 oz*	*2 tbsp*
Snipped chives	*15 ml*	*1 tbsp*	*1 tbsp*

1 Cook the macaroni according to the packet directions. Drain and return to the saucepan.

2 Dry-fry (sauté) the bacon until crisp. Drain on kitchen paper and reserve for garnish.

3 Add the remaining ingredients to the macaroni and toss over a gentle heat until melted. Spoon into warm bowls and sprinkle the bacon over.

PREPARATION TIME: 3 MINUTES

COOKING TIME: 12 MINUTES

Pappardelle Paprikash

You can use up leftover roast lamb or pork in this sauce for a Monday treat. Simply add it with the paprika and continue as below.

SERVES 4	METRIC	IMPERIAL	AMERICAN
Oil	*15 ml*	*1 tbsp*	*1 tbsp*
Onion, chopped	*1*	*1*	*1*
Pork or lamb fillet, finely diced	*225 g*	*8 oz*	*2 cups*
Paprika	*15 ml*	*1 tbsp*	*1 tbsp*
Can of pimientos, drained and sliced	*190 g*	*6¾ oz*	*1 small*
Chicken stock	*150 ml*	*¼ pt*	*⅔ cup*
Pinch of light brown sugar	*1*	*1*	*1*
Salt and white pepper			
Pappardelle	*350 g*	*12 oz*	*12 oz*
Plain (all-purpose) flour	*15 ml*	*1 tbsp*	*1 tbsp*
Water	*15 ml*	*1 tbsp*	*1 tbsp*
Soured (dairy sour) cream	*150 ml*	*¼ pt*	*⅔ cup*
Crisp, fried (sautéed) onion rings, to garnish			

1 Heat the oil in a saucepan and fry (sauté) the onion until softened but not browned.

2 Add the meat and cook, stirring, for 4 minutes.

3 Add the paprika and fry for 1 minute.

4 Add the pimientos and stock. Season with the sugar and a little salt and pepper.

5 Bring to the boil, reduce the heat, half-cover and simmer gently for 15 minutes.

6 Meanwhile, cook the pappardelle according to the packet directions. Drain.

7 Blend the flour with the water and stir into the paprikash sauce. Cook, stirring for 2 minutes. Stir in the cream and heat through. Taste and re-season, if necessary.

8 Spoon the pappardelle on to warm serving plates. Top with the paprikash sauce and garnish with crisp, fried onion rings.

PREPARATION TIME: 5 MINUTES

COOKING TIME: 25 MINUTES

Lamb Goulash Bake

Try this with leftover pork, chicken or turkey.

SERVES 4	METRIC	IMPERIAL	AMERICAN
Elbow macaroni	*225 g*	*8 oz*	*8 oz*
Onion, chopped	*1*	*1*	*1*
Oil	*15 ml*	*1 tbsp*	*1 tbsp*
Can of chopped tomatoes	*400 g*	*14 oz*	*1 large*
Tomato purée (paste)	*15 ml*	*1 tbsp*	*1 tbsp*
Caster (superfine) sugar	*2.5 ml*	*½ tsp*	*½ tsp*
Chicken or beef stock	*150 ml*	*¼ pt*	*⅔ cup*
Paprika	*15 ml*	*1 tbsp*	*1 tbsp*
Cooked lamb, diced	*225 g*	*8 oz*	*8 oz*
Salt and freshly ground black pepper			
Frozen peas or cut green beans	*50 g*	*2 oz*	*2 oz*
Fresh breadcrumbs	*50 g*	*2 oz*	*1 cup*
Caraway seeds	*15 ml*	*1 tbsp*	*1 tbsp*
Butter, melted	*15 g*	*½ oz*	*1 tbsp*
Soured (dairy sour) cream, to serve			

1 Cook the macaroni according to the packet directions. Drain.

2 Fry (sauté) the onion in the oil for 2 minutes until softened slightly but not browned.

3 Add the tomatoes, tomato purée, sugar, stock, paprika, lamb and a little salt and pepper. Bring to the boil, reduce the heat, and simmer gently for about 30 minutes until pulpy and the meat is really tender. Add the peas or beans for the last 5 minutes of cooking time.

4 Taste and re-season, if necessary.

5 Layer in a flameproof dish with the macaroni. Mix the breadcrumbs and caraway seeds with the butter and sprinkle over. Grill (broil) until golden. Serve with soured cream.

PREPARATION TIME: 5 MINUTES

COOKING TIME: 40 MINUTES

Piquant Chicken Liver Vermicelli

Don't serve grated cheese with this sauce, just a cool tomato and onion salad as an accompaniment.

SERVES 4	METRIC	IMPERIAL	AMERICAN
Onions, finely chopped	*2*	*2*	*2*
Butter	*25 g*	*1 oz*	*2 tbsp*
Olive oil	*15 ml*	*1 tbsp*	*1 tbsp*
Wineglass of red vermouth	*1*	*1*	*1*
Chicken livers, trimmed and finely chopped	*450 g*	*1 lb*	*4 cups*
Chopped sage	*5 ml*	*1 tsp*	*1 tsp*
Salt and freshly ground black pepper			
Vermicelli	*225 g*	*8 oz*	*8 oz*
Chopped parsley, to garnish			

1 Fry (sauté) the onions in the butter and oil until softened but not browned.

2 Add the vermouth and simmer until reduced by half.

3 Add the chicken livers and sage and cook quickly, for about 2–3 minutes, until browned but not dry. Season to taste.

4 Meanwhile, cook the vermicelli according to the packet directions. Drain and add to the sauce. Toss over a gentle heat. Pile on to plates and garnish with chopped parsley.

PREPARATION TIME: 10 MINUTES

COOKING TIME: 7–8 MINUTES

Kidney and Mustard Tagliarini

SERVES 4–6	METRIC	IMPERIAL	AMERICAN
Green (spinach) tagliarini	*350 g*	*12 oz*	*12 oz*
Lambs' kidneys	*4*	*4*	*4*
Butter	*40 g*	*1½ oz*	*3 tbsp*
Olive oil	*15 ml*	*1 tbsp*	*1 tbsp*
Brandy	*30 ml*	*2 tbsp*	*2 tbsp*
Dijon or wholegrain mustard	*15 ml*	*1 tbsp*	*1 tbsp*
Double (heavy) cream	*60 ml*	*4 tbsp*	*4 tbsp*
Salt and freshly ground black pepper			
Snipped chives	*30 ml*	*2 tbsp*	*2 tbsp*
Toasted, buttered breadcrumbs, to garnish			

1. Cook the tagliarini according to the packet directions. Drain.
2. Meanwhile, peel off any skin on the kidneys, then cut into halves. Snip out the cores with scissors, then snip the kidneys into small pieces.
3. Heat the butter and oil in a frying pan (skillet). Add the kidneys and cook, stirring, for 2–3 minutes until browned and tender. Do not overcook.
4. Add the brandy and ignite. When the flames die down, add the mustard and cream and heat through, stirring until blended. Season and stir in the chives.
5. Spoon on to the tagliarini and garnish with a sprinkling of toasted buttered breadcrumbs.

PREPARATION TIME: 10 MINUTES

COOKING TIME: 10 MINUTES

Chicken Lasagne

A great way of using up leftover chicken or turkey.

SERVES 6	METRIC	IMPERIAL	AMERICAN
Olive oil	*30 ml*	*2 tbsp*	*2 tbsp*
Large onion, chopped	*1*	*1*	*1*
Garlic clove, crushed	*1*	*1*	*1*
Button mushrooms, sliced	*100 g*	*4 oz*	*4 oz*
Can of chopped tomatoes	*400 g*	*14 oz*	*1 large*
Tomato purée (paste)	*30 ml*	*2 tbsp*	*2 tbsp*
White wine	*60 ml*	*4 tbsp*	*4 tbsp*
Cooked chicken, diced	*225 g*	*8 oz*	*2 cups*
Dried oregano	*5 ml*	*1 tsp*	*1 tsp*
Salt and freshly ground black pepper			
Plain (all-purpose) flour	*20 g*	*¾ oz*	*3 tbsp*
Milk	*300 ml*	*½ pt*	*1¼ cups*
Butter	*15 g*	*½ oz*	*1 tbsp*
Cheddar cheese, grated	*50 g*	*2 oz*	*½ cup*
Grated Parmesan cheese	*30 ml*	*2 tbsp*	*2 tbsp*
Sheets of no-need-to-precook green (spinach) lasagne	*8*	*8*	*8*

1 Heat the oil in a saucepan. Add the onion and garlic and cook for 2 minutes, stirring.

2 Add the mushrooms, tomatoes, tomato purée and wine and simmer for 10 minutes until pulpy.

3 Stir in the chicken and oregano and season to taste.

4 Meanwhile, blend the flour with a little of the milk in a saucepan. Add the remaining milk and the butter.

5 Bring to the boil and cook for 2 minutes, stirring all the time, until thickened and smooth. Stir in the Cheddar cheese and season to taste.

6 Spoon a little of the chicken mixture into the base of a shallow ovenproof dish. Top with a layer of lasagne. Repeat, finishing with a layer of lasagne.

7 Spoon the cheese sauce over and sprinkle with the Parmesan. Bake in a preheated oven at 190°C/375°F/ gas mark 5 for about 35 minutes until golden and the lasagne feels tender when a knife is inserted down through the centre.

PREPARATION TIME: 10 MINUTES

COOKING TIME: 47 MINUTES

Turkey Veronica

You can, of course, use chicken instead of turkey, if you prefer. The only accompaniment needed is a green salad.

SERVES 4	METRIC	IMPERIAL	AMERICAN
Farfalle	*225 g*	*8 oz*	*8 oz*
Butter	*50 g*	*2 oz*	*¼ cup*
Chicken stock	*300 ml*	*½ pt*	*1¼ cups*
Bay leaf	*1*	*1*	*1*
Turkey stir-fry meat	*225 g*	*8 oz*	*8 oz*
Plain (all-purpose) flour	*25 g*	*1 oz*	*¼ cup*
Grated lemon rind	*5 ml*	*1 tsp*	*1 tsp*
Single (light) cream	*150 ml*	*¼ pt*	*⅔ cup*
Seedless white grapes, halved	*75 g*	*3 oz*	*3 oz*
Salt and white pepper			
Chopped parsley, to garnish			

1 Cook the farfalle according to the packet directions. Drain and return to the pan. Add a little of the butter and toss.

2 Meanwhile, put the stock in a pan. Add the bay leaf. Bring to the boil and leave to infuse while preparing the rest of the sauce.

3 Melt the butter in a separate pan. Add the turkey and cook, stirring, for 4–5 minutes until cooked through.

4 Add the flour and cook, stirring, for 1 minute.

5 Discard the bay leaf, then gradually blend the stock into the turkey mixture, stirring all the time. Add the lemon rind. Bring to the boil and cook for 3 minutes, stirring.

6 Stir in the cream, add the grapes and season to taste.

7 Add the farfalle. Toss well and sprinkle with chopped parsley before serving.

PREPARATION TIME: 5 MINUTES

COOKING TIME: 10 MINUTES

Chicken Tetrazzini

SERVES 4	METRIC	IMPERIAL	AMERICAN
Spaghetti	*350 g*	*12 oz*	*12 oz*
Unsalted (sweet) butter	*25 g*	*1 oz*	*2 tbsp*
Garlic clove, crushed	*1*	*1*	*1*
Celery sticks, finely chopped	*2*	*2*	*2*
Bunch of spring onions (scallions), chopped	*1*	*1*	*1*
Button mushrooms, sliced	*225 g*	*8 oz*	*8 oz*
Plain (all-purpose) flour	*45 ml*	*3 tbsp*	*3 tbsp*
Chicken stock	*200 ml*	*7 fl oz*	*scant 1 cup*
Crème fraîche	*250 ml*	*8 fl oz*	*1 cup*
Cooked chicken, roughly diced	*225 g*	*8 oz*	*2 cups*
Parmesan cheese, freshly grated	*50 g*	*2 oz*	*½ cup*
Flaked (slivered) almonds	*30 ml*	*2 tbsp*	*2 tbsp*

1 Cook the spaghetti according to the packet directions. Drain and return to the pan.

2 Meanwhile, melt the butter in a separate pan. Add the garlic, celery, spring onions and mushrooms and cook for 3 minutes, stirring.

3 Stir in the flour and cook for 1 minute. Blend in the stock, bring to the boil and cook for 2 minutes, stirring.

4 Stir in the crème fraîche and cook for 2 minutes. Stir in the chicken.

5 Add to the spaghetti and toss well.

6 Turn into an ovenproof serving dish. Mix the cheese and almonds and sprinkle over.

7 Cook in a preheated oven at 190 °C/375°F/ gas mark 5 for 25 minutes until golden.

PREPARATION TIME:
10 MINUTES

COOKING TIME:
35 MINUTES

Chicken, Leek and Walnut Pasta

An interesting combination of textures and flavours.

SERVES 4	METRIC	IMPERIAL	AMERICAN
Small leeks, thinly sliced	*2*	*2*	*2*
Walnut oil	*15 ml*	*1 tbsp*	*1 tbsp*
Olive oil	*15 ml*	*1 tbsp*	*1 tbsp*
Walnuts, roughly chopped	*50 g*	*2 oz*	*½ cup*
Chicken breast fillets, finely diced	*2*	*2*	*2*
Medium dry white wine	*150 ml*	*¼ pt*	*⅔ cup*
Crème fraîche	*150 ml*	*¼ pt*	*⅔ cup*
Salt and freshly ground black pepper			
Rotelli	*225 g*	*8 oz*	*8 oz*
Chopped parsley, to garnish			

1 Fry (sauté) the leeks in the two types of oil for 2 minutes until slightly softened. Add the walnuts, cover with a lid, reduce the heat and cook gently for 5 minutes until soft.

2 Add the chicken and wine, re-cover and simmer gently for 10 minutes until the chicken is tender.

3 Stir in the crème fraîche and season to taste.

4 Meanwhile, cook the rotelli according to the packet directions. Drain. Add to the sauce. Toss and serve sprinkled with chopped parsley.

PREPARATION TIME: 8 MINUTES

COOKING TIME: 18 MINUTES

SEAFOOD DISHES

Pasta goes well with just about every kind of fish and shellfish from good old canned tuna to more exotic smoked salmon.
In this chapter there are memorable meals for every occasion from the popular Lasagne di Mare to the sophisticated Caviare and Artichoke Prawns.

Spaghetti Alle Vongole

SERVES 4–6	METRIC	IMPERIAL	AMERICAN
Spaghetti	*350 g*	*12 oz*	*12 oz*
Butter	*40 g*	*1½ oz*	*3 tbsp*
Olive oil	*15 ml*	*1 tbsp*	*1 tbsp*
Garlic cloves, crushed	*3*	*3*	*3*
Dry white wine	*100 ml*	*3½ fl oz*	*6½ tbsp*
Cans of baby clams	*2×295 g*	*2×10¾ oz*	*2 small*
Freshly ground black pepper			
Chopped parsley, to garnish			

1 Cook the spaghetti according to the packet directions. Drain.

2 Melt the butter with the oil in a saucepan. Add the garlic and cook gently for 2 minutes until lightly golden but not too brown.

3 Add the wine, bring to the boil and simmer for 2 minutes until slightly reduced.

4 Drain the clams, reserving the juice. Add the clams and 45 ml/3 tbsp of their juice to the saucepan. Heat through gently until piping hot.

5 Add the spaghetti and toss well. Sprinkle with the chopped parsley and serve. Cheese is not served with this dish.

PREPARATION TIME:
3 MINUTES

COOKING TIME:
10 MINUTES

Seafood and Fennel Farfalle

This excellent main course for a supper party will also make an excellent starter for eight people.

SERVES 4	METRIC	IMPERIAL	AMERICAN
Fennel bulb	*1*	*1*	*1*
Olive oil	*45 ml*	*3 tbsp*	*3 tbsp*
Spring onions (scallions), chopped	*8*	*8*	*8*
White wine	*30 ml*	*2 tbsp*	*2 tbsp*
Frozen seafood cocktail, thawed	*225 g*	*8 oz*	*8 oz*
Salt and freshly ground black pepper			
Farfalle (multicoloured, if possible)	*225 g*	*8 oz*	*8 oz*
Lemon twists, to garnish			

1 Finely chop the fennel, reserving the green fronds for garnish.

2 Heat the oil in a saucepan. Add the chopped fennel and spring onions and cook, stirring, for 3 minutes. Cover with a lid and cook gently for 5 minutes until softened.

3 Add the wine and the seafood. Bring to the boil, reduce the heat and cook gently, stirring, for about 3 minutes until hot through. Season to taste with salt and pepper.

4 Meanwhile, cook the farfalle according to the packet directions. Drain. Add to the sauce. Toss and garnish with twists of lemon and the reserved fennel fronds before serving.

PREPARATION TIME: 5 MINUTES

COOKING TIME: 15 MINUTES

Lasagne di Mare

SERVES 4	METRIC	IMPERIAL	AMERICAN
Onion, finely chopped	*1*	*1*	*1*
Garlic clove, crushed	*1*	*1*	*1*
Mushrooms, thinly sliced	*100 g*	*4 oz*	*4 oz*
Can of chopped tomatoes	*400 g*	*14 oz*	*1 large*
Tomato purée (paste)	*15 ml*	*1 tbsp*	*1 tbsp*
Dried oregano	*2.5 ml*	*½ tsp*	*½ tsp*
Cod fillet, skinned and diced	*350 g*	*12 oz*	*12 oz*
Peeled prawns (shrimp)	*100 g*	*4 oz*	*1 cup*
Salt and freshly ground black pepper			
Milk	*600 ml*	*1 pt*	*2½ cups*
Plain (all-purpose) flour	*50 g*	*2 oz*	*½ cup*
Unsalted (sweet) butter	*50 g*	*2 oz*	*¼ cup*
Cheddar cheese, grated	*100 g*	*4 oz*	*1 cup*
Sheet of no-need-to-precook lasagne	*8*	*8*	*8*

1 Put the onion, garlic, mushrooms, tomatoes, tomato purée and oregano in a saucepan. Bring to the boil, reduce the heat and simmer for 15 minutes until thick and pulpy, stirring occasionally.

2 Add the cod and prawns and cook for a further 5 minutes. Season to taste.

3 Blend the flour with a little of the milk in a saucepan. Stir in the remaining milk and add the butter. Bring to the boil and cook for 2 minutes, stirring all the time. Season to taste and stir in half the cheese.

4 Spoon a layer of cheese sauce in the base of a fairly large, shallow, ovenproof dish. Cover with a layer of lasagne, breaking to fit, if necessary.

5 Add a layer of a third of the fish mixture, then a little more cheese sauce. Repeat the layers twice more, making sure there is plenty of cheese sauce to cover the top thickly.

6 Sprinkle with the remaining cheese and cook in a preheated oven at 190°C/375°F/gas mark 5 for about 35 minutes or until golden, bubbling and cooked through.

PREPARATION TIME: 10 MINUTES

COOKING TIME: 57 MINUTES

Sardinian Clams with Bacon

SERVES 4	METRIC	IMPERIAL	AMERICAN
Fusilli	*350 g*	*12 oz*	*12 oz*
Bunch of spring onions (scallions), chopped	*1*	*1*	*1*
Carrot, finely diced	*1*	*1*	*1*
Olive oil	*150 ml*	*¼ pt*	*⅔ cup*
Garlic cloves, crushed	*2*	*2*	*2*
Pancetta, diced	*100 g*	*4 oz*	*4 oz*
Cans of baby clams, drained	*2×295 g*	*2×10¾ oz*	*2 small*
Pinch of cayenne	*1*	*1*	*1*
Chopped thyme	*10 ml*	*2 tsp*	*2 tsp*
Freshly ground black pepper			
Chopped parsley, to garnish			

1. Cook the pasta according to the packet directions. Drain and return to the saucepan.
2. Fry (sauté) the onions and carrot in 60 ml/4 tbsp of the oil for 3 minutes until softened but not browned.
3. Add the garlic and bacon and continue cooking for a further 3 minutes, stirring.
4. Add the remaining oil with the clams, cayenne, thyme and a good grinding of pepper. Heat through gently, stirring, until piping hot.
5. Add to the cooked fusilli. Toss well over a gentle heat. Garnish with chopped parsley before serving.

PREPARATION TIME: 15 MINUTES

COOKING TIME: 10 MINUTES

Tuscan Tuna and Beans

This is a great way of making a little tuna go a long way. It is also very good served cold, spiked with a dash of wine vinegar.

SERVES 6	METRIC	IMPERIAL	AMERICAN
Penne	*225 g*	*8 oz*	*8 oz*
Olive oil	*250 ml*	*8 fl oz*	*1 cup*
Lemon juice	*100 ml*	*3½ fl oz*	*6½ tbsp*
Garlic cloves, crushed	*2*	*2*	*2*
Cans of cannellini beans, drained	*2×425 g*	*2×15 oz*	*2 large*
Chopped parsley	*30 ml*	*2 tbsp*	*2 tbsp*
Can of tuna, drained	*185 g*	*6½ oz*	*1 small*

Salt and freshly ground black pepper

A few black olives, stoned (pitted), and snipped chives, to garnish

1. Cook the pasta according to the packet directions. Drain.
2. Mix the oil, lemon juice, garlic, cannellini beans and parsley together in a saucepan. Cook for 5 minutes, stirring occasionally, until hot through.
3. Gently fold in the tuna, pasta and a little salt and pepper, taking care not to break up the tuna chunks.
4. Toss over a gentle heat, then spoon on to warm plates and garnish with olives and chives.

PREPARATION TIME: 3 MINUTES

COOKING TIME: 10 MINUTES

Tuna with Tomatoes Vesuvius

SERVES 4	METRIC	IMPERIAL	AMERICAN
Orange (sun-dried tomato) tagliatelle	*350 g*	*12 oz*	*12 oz*
Garlic clove, crushed	*1*	*1*	*1*
Chicken stock	*150 ml*	*¼ pt*	*⅔ cup*
Can of chopped tomatoes	*200 g*	*7 oz*	*1 small*
Tomato purée (paste)	*15 ml*	*1 tbsp*	*1 tbsp*
Snipped chives	*30 ml*	*2 tbsp*	*2 tbsp*
Dry vermouth	*45 ml*	*3 tbsp*	*3 tbsp*
Cornflour (cornstarch)	*10 ml*	*2 tsp*	*2 tsp*
Water	*15 ml*	*1 tbsp*	*1 tbsp*
Can of tuna, drained	*185 g*	*6½ oz*	*1 small*
Salt and freshly ground black pepper			
Olive oil	*15 ml*	*1 tbsp*	*1 tbsp*
Single (light) cream, to garnish	*30 ml*	*2 tbsp*	*2 tbsp*

1 Cook the pasta according to the packet directions. Drain and return to the pan.

2 Meanwhile, place the garlic, stock, tomatoes, tomato purée, chives and vermouth in a saucepan. Bring to the boil, reduce the heat and simmer for 5 minutes or until reduced by half.

3 Add the tuna and heat through, stirring.

4 Blend the cornflour with the water. Add to the sauce, bring to the boil and simmer for 1 minute, stirring.

5 Season to taste and stir in the olive oil.

6 Add the single cream to the tagliatelle and heat through gently. Sprinkle well with black pepper. Pile on to plates and spoon the sauce on top.

PREPARATION TIME: 3 MINUTES

COOKING TIME: 12 MINUTES

Quick Crab Creation

This dish tastes equally delicious with prawns (shrimp) instead of crabsticks.

SERVES 4	METRIC	IMPERIAL	AMERICAN
Conchiglie	*225 g*	*8 oz*	*8 oz*
Crabsticks, diced	*225 g*	*8 oz*	*8 oz*
Can of crab bisque	*425 g*	*15 oz*	*1 large*
Single (light) cream	*30 ml*	*2 tbsp*	*2 tbsp*
Salt and freshly ground black pepper			
Chopped parsley	*30 ml*	*2 tbsp*	*2 tbsp*
A little lemon juice (optional)			
Stuffed olives, sliced, to garnish			

1 Cook the pasta according to the packet directions. Drain and return to the pan.

2 Mix in the crabsticks, soup and cream.

3 Heat through gently until hot. Season to taste and stir in the parsley. Sprinkle with lemon juice, if liked.

4 Spoon on to warm plates and garnish with olives.

PREPARATION TIME: 3 MINUTES

COOKING TIME: 10 MINUTES

Cheesy Tuna and Sweetcorn Grill

A storecupboard favourite with all the family.

SERVES 4	METRIC	IMPERIAL	AMERICAN
Conchiglie	*225 g*	*8 oz*	*8 oz*
Plain (all-purpose) flour	*20 g*	*¾ oz*	*3 tbsp*
Butter	*20 g*	*¾ oz*	*1½ tbsp*
Milk	*300 ml*	*½ pt*	*1¼ cups*
Strong Cheddar cheese, grated	*50 g*	*2 oz*	*½ cup*
Salt and freshly ground black pepper			
Can of tuna, drained	*185 g*	*6½ oz*	*1 small*
Can of sweetcorn (corn), drained	*200 g*	*7 oz*	*1 small*
Chopped parsley	*15 ml*	*1 tbsp*	*1 tbsp*
A little grated cheese, to garnish			

1 Cook the pasta according to the packet directions. Drain.

2 Meanwhile, whisk the flour, butter and milk together in a saucepan until the flour is well blended in. Bring to the boil, stirring all the time, until thickened and smooth. Simmer for 2 minutes.

3 Add the cooked pasta and the remaining ingredients and heat through, stirring, until piping hot.

4 Turn into a flameproof dish. Sprinkle with a little more grated cheese and grill (broil) until golden and bubbling.

PREPARATION TIME:
5 MINUTES

COOKING TIME:
15 MINUTES

Mussel Magic

SERVES 4–6	METRIC	IMPERIAL	AMERICAN
Mussels in their shells	*2 kg*	*4½ lb*	*4½ lb*
Olive oil	*120 ml*	*4 fl oz*	*½ cup*
Garlic cloves, crushed	*3*	*3*	*3*
Chicken stock	*150 ml*	*¼ pt*	*⅔ cup*
Brandy	*15 ml*	*1 tbsp*	*1 tbsp*
Chopped parsley	*30 ml*	*2 tbsp*	*2 tbsp*
Salt and freshly ground black pepper			
Vermicelli	*225 g*	*8 oz*	*8 oz*

1 Scrub the mussels, discard the beards and any shells that are open, damaged or don't close when tapped.

2 Heat 45 ml/3 tbsp of the oil in a large pan. Add the garlic and fry (sauté) gently until golden.

3 Add the mussels and the stock. Cover and cook gently for 3–4 minutes, shaking the pan occasionally until the mussels have opened.

4 Strain the liquid into a clean pan. Carefully remove the mussels from their shells and add to the liquid.

5 Stir in the brandy and parsley and season to taste. Reheat gently.

6 Meanwhile, cook the vermicelli according to the packet directions. Drain and add to the sauce. Heat through, tossing gently.

PREPARATION TIME:
20 MINUTES

COOKING TIME:
8 MINUTES

Fiery Mussel Capellini

SERVES 4	METRIC	IMPERIAL	AMERICAN
Capellini	*225 g*	*8 oz*	*8 oz*
Olive oil	*30 ml*	*2 tbsp*	*2 tbsp*
Onion, finely chopped	*1*	*1*	*1*
Garlic clove, crushed	*1*	*1*	*1*
Red chilli, seeded and chopped	*1*	*1*	*1*
Canned pimiento caps, roughly chopped	*2*	*2*	*2*
Can of chopped tomatoes	*400 g*	*14 oz*	*1 large*
Tomato purée (paste)	*15 ml*	*1 tbsp*	*1 tbsp*
Can of mussels, drained	*250 g*	*9 oz*	*1 small*
Salt and freshly ground black pepper			

1. Cook the capellini according to the packet directions. Drain.
2. Meanwhile, heat the oil in a saucepan. Add the onion and garlic and cook gently for about 2 minutes until softened but not browned.
3. Add the chilli, pimientos, tomatoes and tomato purée. Bring to the boil, reduce the heat and simmer gently for 10 minutes until pulpy.
4. Stir in the mussels and capellini. Season to taste and toss over a gentle heat until piping hot.

PREPARATION TIME:
10 MINUTES

COOKING TIME:
14 MINUTES

Caviare and Artichoke Prawns

SERVES 4	METRIC	IMPERIAL	AMERICAN
Farfalle	*225 g*	*8 oz*	*8 oz*
Olive oil	*45 ml*	*3 tbsp*	*3 tbsp*
Onion, finely chopped	*1*	*1*	*1*
Dry white vermouth	*45 ml*	*3 tbsp*	*3 tbsp*
Can of artichoke hearts, drained and chopped	*425 g*	*15 oz*	*1 large*
Peeled prawns (shrimp)	*100 g*	*4 oz*	*1 cup*
Green olives, stoned (pitted) and halved	*6*	*6*	*6*
Freshly ground black pepper			
Snipped chives	*15 ml*	*1 tbsp*	*1 tbsp*
Jar of Danish lumpfish roe, to garnish	*50 g*	*2 oz*	*1 small*

1 Cook the farfalle according to the packet directions. Drain.

2 Heat the oil, add the onion and fry (sauté) gently for 3 minutes until softened but not browned.

3 Add the vermouth, bring to the boil and simmer for 1 minute.

4 Add the pasta, artichokes, prawns, olives and a good grinding of pepper. Heat through, stirring gently, until piping hot. Add the chives.

5 Spoon on to warm plates and top each portion with a spoonful of lumpfish roe.

PREPARATION TIME: 10 MINUTES

COOKING TIME: 10 MINUTES

Prawn and Courgette Bake

This recipe is also good with diced crabsticks instead of the prawns (shrimp).

SERVES 4–6	METRIC	IMPERIAL	AMERICAN
Lumachi	*225 g*	*8 oz*	*8 oz*
Butter	*50 g*	*2 oz*	*¼ cup*
Bunch of spring onions (scallions), chopped	*1*	*1*	*1*
Courgettes (zucchini), sliced	*2*	*2*	*2*
Fish stock	*450 ml*	*¾ pt*	*2 cups*
Dry cider	*150 ml*	*¼ pt*	*⅔ cup*
Cornflour (cornstarch)	*45 ml*	*3 tbsp*	*3 tbsp*
Peeled prawns	*175 g*	*6 oz*	*1½ cups*
Chopped parsley	*15 ml*	*1 tbsp*	*1 tbsp*
Salt and white pepper			
Single (light) cream	*150 ml*	*¼ pt*	*⅔ cup*
Branflakes, crushed	*50 g*	*2 oz*	*1 cup*

1 Cook the lumachi according to the packet directions. Drain.

2 Meanwhile, melt the butter in a saucepan. Add the spring onions and courgettes and fry (sauté) gently for 2 minutes. Cover and cook for 5 minutes until softened but not browned, stirring occasionally.

3 Add the stock and bring to the boil. Simmer for 2 minutes.

4 Blend the cider with the cornflour and stir into the mixture. Bring to the boil and simmer for 1 minute, stirring all the time.

5 Stir in the pasta, prawns, a little salt and pepper and the cream.

6 Turn into an ovenproof dish and top with the branflakes. Bake in a preheated oven at 190°C/385°F/ gas mark 5 for about 20 minutes until bubbling.

PREPARATION TIME: 10 MINUTES

COOKING TIME: 30 MINUTES

Mediterranean Salt Cod

Remember to soak the cod for 24 hours before use.

SERVES 4	METRIC	IMPERIAL	AMERICAN
Salt cod, soaked overnight in cold water	*450 g*	*1 lb*	*1 lb*
Lemon juice	*15 ml*	*1 tbsp*	*1 tbsp*
Plain (all-purpose) flour	*50 g*	*2 oz*	*½ cup*
Oil for shallow frying			
Olive oil	*30 ml*	*2 tbsp*	*2 tbsp*
Garlic clove, crushed	*1*	*1*	*1*
Onion, chopped	*1*	*1*	*1*
Can of chopped tomatoes	*400 g*	*14 oz*	*1 large*
Tomato purée (paste)	*15 ml*	*1 tbsp*	*1 tbsp*
Caster (superfine) sugar	*5 ml*	*1 tsp*	*1 tsp*
Green stuffed olives	*12*	*12*	*12*
Cocktail gherkins (cornichons), halved lengthways	*6*	*6*	*6*
Capers	*10 ml*	*2 tsp*	*2 tsp*
Chopped parsley	*15 ml*	*1 tbsp*	*1 tbsp*
Fettucci	*350 g*	*12 oz*	*12 oz*
Lemon wedges, to garnish			

1 Drain the soaked cod. Place in a saucepan and cover with cold water and lemon juice. Bring to the boil, part-cover and boil for 5 minutes. Drain and repeat until the fish is tender.

2 Remove the skin and any bones and break the fish into bite-sized pieces. Dust with flour. Shallow-fry (sauté) until golden brown. Drain on kitchen paper.

3 Meanwhile, heat half the olive oil in a saucepan. Fry the garlic and onion for 3 minutes until softened but not browned. Add the tomatoes, tomato purée and sugar. Bring to the boil, reduce the heat and simmer for 10 minutes until pulpy.

4 Stir in the cod, olives, gherkins and capers. Simmer gently for 3 minutes. Stir in the parsley.

5 Meanwhile, cook the fettucci according to the packet directions. Drain and toss in the remaining olive oil.

6 Pile the pasta on to warm plates and spoon the cod and sauce over. Garnish with wedges of lemon.

PREPARATION TIME:
8 MINUTES
PLUS SOAKING TIME

COOKING TIME:
30 MINUTES

Brandied Crab Supper

Crab Thermidor is a very rich dish. Serving the mixture as a sauce with pasta offsets this and makes it a perfect party dish.

SERVES 4–6	METRIC	IMPERIAL	AMERICAN
Penne	*225 g*	*8 oz*	*8 oz*
Plain (all-purpose) flour	*25 g*	*1 oz*	*¼ cup*
Butter	*25 g*	*1 oz*	*2 tbsp*
Milk	*300 ml*	*½ pt*	*1¼ cups*
Single (light) cream	*30 ml*	*2 tbsp*	*2 tbsp*
Cheddar cheese, grated	*50 g*	*2 oz*	*½ cup*
Dijon mustard	*5 ml*	*1 tsp*	*1 tsp*
Dried thyme	*2.5 ml*	*½ tsp*	*½ tsp*
Salt and freshly ground black pepper			
Brandy	*15 ml*	*1 tbsp*	*1 tbsp*
Cans of white crabmeat	*2×170 g*	*2×6 oz*	*2 small*
Toasted, buttered breadcrumbs and freshly grated Parmesan cheese, to garnish			

1. Cook the penne according to the packet directions. Drain.
2. Meanwhile, whisk the flour, butter and milk together in a saucepan until the flour is blended in.
3. Bring to the boil and cook for 2 minutes, stirring all the time.
4. Stir in the cream, cheese, mustard and thyme. Season with a little salt and pepper.

5 Add the brandy and the contents of both cans of crabmeat, including the juice. Stir in gently. Add the pasta.

6 Heat through until piping hot. Taste and re-season, if necessary.

7 Turn into a flameproof dish. Sprinkle with buttered breadcrumbs and a little Parmesan. Flash under a hot grill (broiler) until bubbling.

PREPARATION TIME: 5 MINUTES

COOKING TIME: 12 MINUTES

Cod and Rigatoni Ragu

SERVES 4–6	METRIC	IMPERIAL	AMERICAN
Rigatoni	*225 g*	*8 oz*	*8 oz*
Onion, chopped	*1*	*1*	*1*
Garlic clove, crushed	*1*	*1*	*1*
Olive oil	*15 ml*	*1 tbsp*	*1 tbsp*
Button mushrooms, sliced	*100 g*	*4 oz*	*4 oz*
Can of chopped tomatoes	*400 g*	*14 oz*	*1 large*
Tomato purée (paste)	*15 ml*	*1 tbsp*	*1 tbsp*
Frozen peas	*50 g*	*2 oz*	*2 oz*
Chopped basil leaves	*15 ml*	*1 tbsp*	*1 tbsp*
Salt and freshly ground black pepper			
Cod fillet, skinned and diced	*450 g*	*1 lb*	*1 lb*
A few extra basil leaves, to garnish			
Grated Cheddar cheese, to serve			

1. Cook the rigatoni according to the packet directions. Drain.
2. Meanwhile, fry (sauté) the onion and garlic in the oil for 2 minutes until softened but not browned.
3. Add the remaining ingredients except the cod. Bring to the boil, then simmer for 10 minutes until pulpy.
4. Add the fish and cook for a further 5 minutes, stirring gently occasionally, until the fish is cooked.
5. Fold in the pasta. Pile on to warm plates, garnish with basil leaves and serve with grated Cheddar cheese.

PREPARATION TIME:
10 MINUTES

COOKING TIME:
17 MINUTES

Scallop and Bacon Wheels

SERVES 4–6	METRIC	IMPERIAL	AMERICAN
Wholewheat ruote	*225 g*	*8 oz*	*8 oz*
Small leeks, sliced	*2*	*2*	*2*
Butter	*25 g*	*1 oz*	*2 tbsp*
Fish stock	*90 ml*	*6 tbsp*	*6 tbsp*
Streaky bacon rashers (slices)	*4*	*4*	*4*
Baby scallops	*175 g*	*6 oz*	*6 oz*
Fromage frais	*50 g*	*2 oz*	*¼ cup*
Salt and freshly ground black pepper			
Chopped parsley, to garnish			

1 Cook the ruote according to the packet directions. Drain.

2 Fry (sauté) the leeks in half the butter for 2 minutes until softened but not browned.

3 Add the stock, cover and simmer gently for about 5 minutes until tender. Purée in a blender or food processor, then return to the saucepan. Stir in the pasta and heat through.

4 Meanwhile, dry-fry the bacon until the fat runs. Add the scallops and toss for 2 minutes until cooked.

5 Stir the fromage frais into the leek and pasta mixture. Season to taste and heat through.

6 Pile on to plates and top with the bacon and scallops. Sprinkle with chopped parsley before serving.

PREPARATION TIME:
10 MINUTES

COOKING TIME:
12 MINUTES

Country Cod and Vegetable Pasta Casserole

Try using different mixtures of frozen vegetables in this useful storecupboard standby.

SERVES 6	METRIC	IMPERIAL	AMERICAN
Fish or vegetable stock	*300 ml*	*½ pt*	*1¼ cups*
Tomato ketchup (catsup)	*60 ml*	*4 tbsp*	*4 tbsp*
Mayonnaise (not salad cream)	*30 ml*	*2 tbsp*	*2 tbsp*
Frozen mixed country vegetables	*350 g*	*12 oz*	*12 oz*
Salt and pepper			
Frozen cod fillet, thawed, skinned and cubed	*450 g*	*1 lb*	*1 lb*
Dried mixed herbs	*2.5 ml*	*½ tsp*	*½ tsp*
Fettuccine	*350 g*	*12 oz*	*12 oz*
Cheddar cheese, grated	*50 g*	*2 oz*	*½ cup*

1 Mix the stock, ketchup and mayonnaise together in a saucepan. Add the vegetables and a little seasoning, cover and simmer for 10 minutes or until tender.

2 Add the fish and herbs.

3 Meanwhile, cook the fettuccine according to the packet directions. Drain and turn into a large flameproof casserole.

4 Spoon the fish and vegetable mixture over and sprinkle with the cheese. Bake in a preheated oven at 190°C/375°F/gas mark 5 for about 25 minutes until golden and cooked through.

PREPARATION TIME: 3 MINUTES

COOKING TIME: 40 MINUTES

Tagliatelle alla Rustica

This sauce complements fresh tagliatelle perfectly.

SERVES 4	METRIC	IMPERIAL	AMERICAN
Orange (tomato) or green (spinach) tagliatelle	*350 g*	*12 oz*	*12 oz*
Garlic cloves, crushed	*2*	*2*	*2*
Olive oil	*90 ml*	*6 tbsp*	*6 tbsp*
Can of anchovy fillets, chopped, reserving the oil	*50 g*	*2 oz*	*1 small*
Dried oregano	*5 ml*	*1 tsp*	*1 tsp*
Salt and freshly ground black pepper			
Roughly chopped parsley and fresh Parmesan cheese, shaved from a block with a potato peeler, to garnish			

1 Cook the tagliatelle according to the packet directions (or see page 157).

2 Fry (sauté) the garlic in the oil until golden brown.

3 Remove from the heat and add the anchovies and their oil. Return to the heat and cook gently, stirring, until the anchovies form a paste.

4 Stir in the oregano, a very little salt and lots of black pepper.

5 Add to the freshly cooked tagliatelle and toss well. Sprinkle with the parsley and the shavings of Parmesan.

PREPARATION TIME: 5 MINUTES

COOKING TIME: 6–8 MINUTES

Roman Squid and Radicchio

SERVES 4	METRIC	IMPERIAL	AMERICAN
Olive oil	*60 ml*	*4 tbsp*	*4 tbsp*
Garlic cloves, crushed	*2*	*2*	*2*
Red onion, chopped	*1*	*1*	*1*
Green (bell) pepper, finely chopped	*½*	*½*	*½*
Baby squid, cleaned and sliced into rings	*450 g*	*1 lb*	*1 lb*
Salt and freshly ground black pepper			
Lemon juice	*30 ml*	*2 tbsp*	*2 tbsp*
Small head of radicchio, torn into bite-sized pieces	*1*	*1*	*1*
Chopped parsley	*15 ml*	*1 tbsp*	*1 tbsp*
Pappardelle	*350 g*	*12 oz*	*12 oz*
Unsalted (sweet) butter	*25 g*	*1 oz*	*2 tbsp*

1 Heat the oil in a large frying pan (skillet) and fry (sauté) the garlic, onion and pepper for 3 minutes, stirring until softened but not browned.

2 Add the squid, season well with salt and pepper and add the lemon juice. Stir-fry for 1 minute, then cover and cook gently for 5 minutes.

3 Add the radicchio and cook, stirring, for 2 minutes until slightly wilted. Sprinkle with chopped parsley and heat through for a further minute.

4 Cook the pappardelle according to the packet directions. Drain. Add the butter and toss. Spoon on to plates and top with the hot sauce. Serve at once.

PREPARATION TIME:
15 MINUTES

COOKING TIME:
15 MINUTES

Smoked Salmon, Egg and Broccoli Tagliatelle

Look for smoked salmon pieces, which are much cheaper than slices.

SERVES 4	METRIC	IMPERIAL	AMERICAN
Plain or orange (tomato) tagliatelle	*350 g*	*12 oz*	*12 oz*
Broccoli, cut into tiny florets	*225 g*	*8 oz*	*8 oz*
Smoked salmon, cut into small pieces	*100 g*	*4 oz*	*4 oz*
Crème fraîche	*300 ml*	*½ pt*	*1¼ cups*
Chopped dill (dill weed)	*15 ml*	*1 tbsp*	*1 tbsp*
Hard-boiled (hard-cooked) eggs, roughly chopped	*2*	*2*	*2*
Salt and freshly ground black pepper			
A little butter and a few small sprigs of dill, to garnish			

1 Cook the tagliatelle according to the packet directions, adding the broccoli for the last 4 minutes' cooking time. Drain and return to the pan.

2 Add the remaining ingredients and heat through gently, stirring lightly until piping hot.

3 Pile on to warm plates. Top with flakes of butter and small sprigs of dill.

PREPARATION TIME:
8 MINUTES

COOKING TIME:
8 MINUTES

Smoked Haddock Bake

You can, of course, use any smoked fish for this recipe. It is also good with plain white fish.

SERVES 4	METRIC	IMPERIAL	AMERICAN
Elbow macaroni	*225 g*	*8 oz*	*8 oz*
Smoked haddock fillet	*225 g*	*8 oz*	*8 oz*
Milk	*450 ml*	*¾ pt*	*2 cups*
Bay leaf	*1*	*1*	*1*
Butter	*25 g*	*1 oz*	*2 tbsp*
Button mushrooms, sliced	*100 g*	*4 oz*	*4 oz*
Plain (all-purpose) flour	*25 g*	*1 oz*	*¼ cup*
Cheddar cheese, grated	*100 g*	*4 oz*	*1 cup*
Salt and white pepper			
Warmed passata (sieved tomatoes), to serve			

1 Cook the macaroni according to the packet directions. Drain.

2 Meanwhile, poach the fish in the milk, with the bay leaf added, for 5 minutes or until it flakes easily with a fork.

3 Reserve the milk. Discard the skin and any bones from the fish and break into bite-sized pieces.

4 Melt the butter in the saucepan, add the mushrooms and cook gently, stirring for 1 minute.

5 Add the flour and cook for 1 further minute.

6 Remove from the heat and gradually blend in the reserved milk, discarding the bay leaf. Return to the heat, bring to the boil and cook for 2 minutes, stirring. Stir in half the cheese and season to taste. Gently fold in the fish and pasta and reheat until piping hot.

7 Spoon into a flameproof dish, sprinkle with the remaining grated cheese and flash under a hot grill (broiler) to brown the top. Serve with warmed passata handed separately.

PREPARATION TIME: 5 MINUTES

COOKING TIME: 15 MINUTES

Salmon with Pimientos and Basil

For a quick supper dish, use a can of salmon instead of the fillet. Take care not to break the fish up too much when you remove the skin and bones.

SERVES 4	METRIC	IMPERIAL	AMERICAN
Wholewheat ruote	*225 g*	*8 oz*	*8 oz*
Salmon fillet, skinned and cut into thin strips	*225 g*	*8 oz*	*8 oz*
Grated rind and juice of ½ lemon			
Olive oil	*150 ml*	*¼ pt*	*⅔ cup*
Spring onions (scallions), chopped	*8*	*8*	*8*
Can of pimientos, drained and cut into strips	*400 g*	*14 oz*	*1 large*
Chopped basil	*15 ml*	*1 tbsp*	*1 tbsp*
Salt and freshly ground black pepper			
Toasted, buttered breadcrumbs and a few torn basil leaves, to garnish			

1 Cook the ruote according to the packet directions. Drain and return to the pan.

2 Meanwhile, put the salmon in a dish with the lemon rind and juice and leave to marinate while preparing the rest of the sauce.

3 Heat 60 ml/4 tbsp of the oil in a saucepan and fry (sauté) the spring onions for about 3 minutes, until softened but not browned.

4 Add the pimientos and toss in the oil for 2 minutes.

5 Add the salmon with any juices and cook gently for 2 minutes until just cooked – do not overcook.

6 Add the basil and remaining oil and season well with salt and pepper. Heat through until piping hot.

7 Add immediately to the cooked wholewheat ruote and toss well. Serve very hot, sprinkled with the toasted breadcrumbs and a few torn basil leaves.

PREPARATION TIME:
15 MINUTES

COOKING TIME:
10–15 MINUTES

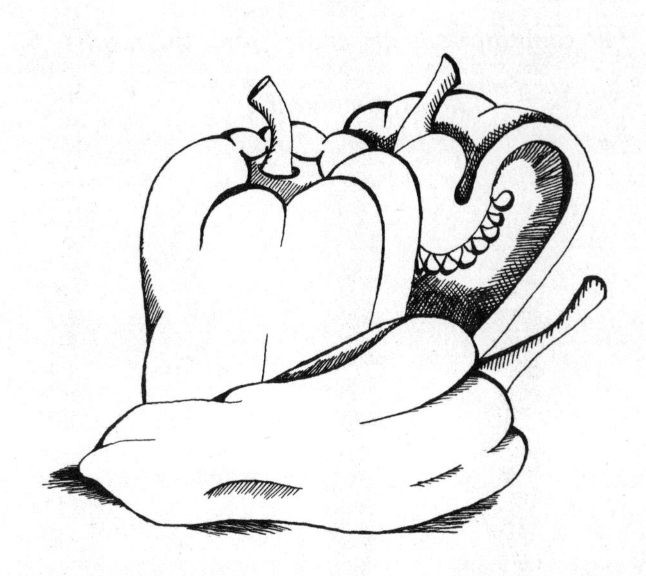

VEGETABLE DISHES

The glorious colours and flavours of vegetables with pasta make them ideal as main meals in their own right, or they can be served as a starter or an accompaniment to fish or meat (when they'll serve more people). The combinations are endless and the results always rewarding.

Tagliarini Primavera

SERVES 4	METRIC	IMPERIAL	AMERICAN
Tagliarini	*350 g*	*12 oz*	*12 oz*
Bunch of spring onions (scallions), chopped	*1*	*1*	*1*
Carrots, cut into short matchsticks	*2*	*2*	*2*
Leeks, cut into short matchsticks	*2*	*2*	*2*
Mangetout (snow peas)	*50 g*	*2 oz*	*2 oz*
Baby corn cobs, halved if long	*50 g*	*2 oz*	*2 oz*
Asparagus tips, halved	*100 g*	*4 oz*	*4 oz*
Dry white wine	*60 ml*	*4 tbsp*	*4 tbsp*
Crème fraîche	*250 ml*	*8 fl oz*	*1 cup*
Salt and freshly ground black pepper			
Chopped parsley	*15 ml*	*1 tbsp*	*1 tbsp*
Paprika, to garnish			
Shavings of fresh Parmesan, to serve			

1 Cook the tagliarini according to the packet directions. Drain and return to the saucepan.

2 Meanwhile, cook the prepared vegetables in boiling, lightly salted water for 3 minutes. Drain.

3 Put the wine and crème fraîche in a pan and boil for 5 minutes until reduced and thickened. Add the drained vegetables and parsley and season to taste.

4 Toss the sauce with the pasta over a gentle heat.

5 Pile on to warm plates and sprinkle with paprika. Serve with shavings of fresh Parmesan.

PREPARATION TIME: 15 MINUTES

COOKING TIME: 12 MINUTES

Spinach and Ricotta Ravioli

SERVES 4–6	METRIC	IMPERIAL	AMERICAN
Plain (all-purpose) flour	*450 g*	*1 lb*	*4 cups*
Salt	*1.5 ml*	*¼ tsp*	*¼ tsp*
Eggs, beaten	*5*	*5*	*5*
Milk	*30 ml*	*2 tbsp*	*2 tbsp*
Spinach, cooked, thoroughly drained and chopped	*225 g*	*8 oz*	*8 oz*
Chopped basil	*15 ml*	*1 tbsp*	*1 tbsp*
Ricotta cheese	*100 g*	*4 oz*	*½ cup*
Freshly ground black pepper			
Tomato sauce (see Tagliatelle alla Salsa di Pomodoro page 110)			

1 Sift the flour and salt into a bowl. Make a well in the centre and add four of the eggs and the milk.

2 Gradually work together to form a dough, then knead gently on a lightly floured surface until smooth. Cover with clingfilm (plastic wrap) and leave to stand for 30 minutes.

3 Roll out as thinly as possible on a lightly floured surface to a large rectangle and cut in half. Lay each half on a clean cloth over the back of a chair and leave for 10 minutes.

4 Meanwhile, beat the spinach with the basil, the remaining egg, the Ricotta, a little salt and lots of pepper.

5 Lay one sheet of pasta on the work surface. Put teaspoonfuls of the mixture at regular intervals in rows on the pasta. Brush with water all round each pile of filling.

6 Lay the second sheet of pasta on top and press gently between each mound of filling. Using a pastry wheel or knife, cut between the piles of filling down the length, then across in rows to form little cushions of filled pasta.

7 Bring a large pan of salted water to the boil. Drop in the ravioli and cook for 8 minutes until just tender.

8 Remove from the pan with a draining spoon and place in warm bowls. Spoon the tomato sauce over and serve.

PREPARATION TIME:
40 MINUTES
PLUS STANDING TIME

COOKING TIME:
8 MINUTES

Spaghettini Rosmarino

Some versions of this dish do not have tomatoes. So, if you prefer, omit them and cook the sauce for 5 minutes only.

SERVES 4	METRIC	IMPERIAL	AMERICAN
Olive oil	*60 ml*	*4 tbsp*	*4 tbsp*
Onion, finely chopped	*1*	*1*	*1*
Garlic cloves, crushed	*2–3*	*2–3*	*2–3*
Chopped rosemary	*20 ml*	*4 tsp*	*4 tsp*
Chopped parsley	*15 ml*	*1 tbsp*	*1 tbsp*
Tomatoes, skinned and chopped	*3*	*3*	*3*
Lime juice	*45 ml*	*3 tbsp*	*3 tbsp*
Salt and freshly ground black pepper			
Spaghettini	*350 g*	*12 oz*	*12 oz*

1 Heat the oil in a saucepan and add the onion, garlic, rosemary, parsley and tomatoes. Simmer for 10 minutes, stirring occasionally.

2 Purée in a blender or food processor. Return to the pan and add the lime juice, salt and freshly ground black pepper to taste.

3 Meanwhile, cook the spaghettini according to the packet directions. Drain and return to the pan.

4 Add the sauce, toss well over a gentle heat, then pile on to warm plates and serve straight away.

PREPARATION TIME:
8 MINUTES

COOKING TIME:
12 MINUTES

Piquant Red Lentil and Tomato Pot

SERVES 4	METRIC	IMPERIAL	AMERICAN
Red lentils	*225 g*	*8 oz*	*1⅓ cups*
Can of chopped tomatoes	*400 g*	*14 oz*	*1 large*
Can of pimientos, drained and chopped	*200 g*	*7 oz*	*1 small*
Dried mixed herbs	*5 ml*	*1 tsp*	*1 tsp*
Tomato purée (paste)	*15 ml*	*1 tbsp*	*1 tbsp*
Caster (superfine) sugar	*5 ml*	*1 tsp*	*1 tsp*
Tabasco sauce			
Salt and freshly ground black pepper			
Chopped parsley	*15 ml*	*1 tbsp*	*1 tbsp*
Multi-coloured penne	*225 g*	*8 oz*	*8 oz*
Olive oil and freshly grated Parmesan cheese, to garnish			

1 Boil the lentils in salted water for 20 minutes, drain and return to the saucepan.

2 Add the tomatoes, pimientos, herbs, tomato purée, sugar and a good sprinkling of Tabasco. Bring to the boil and simmer for about 10 minutes until pulpy. Season to taste and stir in the parsley.

3 Meanwhile, cook the pasta according to the packet directions. Drain and toss in a little olive oil.

4 Add the sauce, toss again and serve with plenty of grated Parmesan sprinkled over.

PREPARATION TIME:
3 MINUTES

COOKING TIME:
20 MINUTES

Spaghetti di Napoli

A popular variation for meat-eaters is to add 100 g/4 oz chopped bacon or pancetta when cooking the onion and green pepper mixture.

SERVES 4	METRIC	IMPERIAL	AMERICAN
Garlic cloves, crushed	*2*	*2*	*2*
Chopped basil	*10 ml*	*2 tsp*	*2 tsp*
Bay leaf	*1*	*1*	*1*
Olive oil	*15 ml*	*1 tbsp*	*1 tbsp*
Red wine	*90 ml*	*6 tbsp*	*6 tbsp*
Plum tomatoes, skinned and chopped	*4*	*4*	*4*
Tomato purée (paste)	*30 ml*	*2 tbsp*	*2 tbsp*
Unsalted (sweet) butter	*25 g*	*1 oz*	*2 tbsp*
Large green (bell) peppers, finely chopped	*2*	*2*	*2*
Large red onion, finely chopped	*1*	*1*	*1*
Button mushrooms, sliced	*225 g*	*8 oz*	*8 oz*
Cornflour (cornstarch)	*10 ml*	*2 tsp*	*2 tsp*
Water	*15 ml*	*1 tbsp*	*1 tbsp*
Salt and freshly ground black pepper			
Spaghetti	*350 g*	*12 oz*	*12 oz*
A few torn basil leaves, to garnish			

1 Put the garlic, chopped basil, bay leaf and oil in a pan and cook for 1 minute.

2 Add the wine, tomatoes and tomato purée. Bring to the boil, reduce the heat and cook gently for 15 minutes until pulpy.

3 Meanwhile, melt half the butter in a frying pan (skillet) and fry (sauté) the peppers and onion for 5 minutes until softened, stirring all the time.

4 Add the mushrooms, stir, cover and cook gently for 5 minutes, stirring occasionally, until the mixture is cooked through. Add to the tomato mixture.

5 Blend the cornflour with the water and stir into the mixture. Cook, stirring, for 2 minutes. Discard the bay leaf and season to taste.

6 Meanwhile, cook the spaghetti according to the packet directions. Drain and toss in the remaining butter.

7 Pile on to plates, spoon the sauce over and scatter a few torn basil leaves over before serving.

PREPARATION TIME: 10 MINUTES

COOKING TIME: 28 MINUTES

Tuono e Lampo

SERVES 4	METRIC	IMPERIAL	AMERICAN
Rotelli	*225 g*	*8 oz*	*8 oz*
Onion, finely chopped	*1*	*1*	*1*
Garlic clove, crushed	*1*	*1*	*1*
Olive oil	*30 ml*	*2 tbsp*	*2 tbsp*
Can of chick peas (garbanzos), drained	*430 g*	*15½ oz*	*1 large*
Dried oregano	*5 ml*	*1 tsp*	*1 tsp*
Passata (sieved tomatoes)	*450 ml*	*¾ pt*	*2 cups*
Tomato purée (paste)	*30 ml*	*2 tbsp*	*2 tbsp*
Caster (superfine) sugar	*5 ml*	*1 tsp*	*1 tsp*
Salt and freshly ground black pepper			
Chopped basil	*15 ml*	*1 tbsp*	*1 tbsp*
Pecorino cheese, grated	*75 g*	*3 oz*	*¾ cup*
A few stoned (pitted) green and black olives, halved, to garnish			

1 Cook the pasta according to the packet directions. Drain.

2 Meanwhile, fry (sauté) the onion and garlic in the oil for 3 minutes, stirring.

3 Add the chick peas and oregano and cook gently for a further 5 minutes.

4 Add to the pasta and toss well over a gentle heat.

5 Meanwhile, put the passata in a pan with the tomato purée, sugar and a little salt and pepper and simmer gently for 10 minutes, stirring occasionally, until thickened. Stir in the chopped basil and half the cheese.

6 Spoon the sauce over the pasta mixture. Sprinkle with the remaining cheese and the olives.

PREPARATION TIME: 5 MINUTES

COOKING TIME: 12–15 MINUTES

Walnut and Broccoli Sensation

SERVES 4	METRIC	IMPERIAL	AMERICAN
Green (spinach) tagliatelle	*350 g*	*12 oz*	*12 oz*
Broccoli, cut into tiny florets	*225 g*	*8 oz*	*8 oz*
Mayonnaise	*120 ml*	*4 fl oz*	*½ cup*
Fromage frais	*120 ml*	*4 fl oz*	*½ cup*
Walnuts, coarsely chopped	*25 g*	*1 oz*	*¼ cup*
Dijon mustard	*5 ml*	*1 tsp*	*1 tsp*
Salt and freshly ground black pepper			

1 Cook the tagliatelle according to the packet directions. Drain.

2 Cook the broccoli in boiling, lightly salted water for 4 minutes. Drain and return to the saucepan.

3 Add the mayonnaise, fromage frais, walnuts and mustard. Season with salt and pepper and heat through gently.

4 Add the cooked tagliatelle to the sauce and toss over a gentle heat. Serve straight away.

PREPARATION TIME: 5 MINUTES

COOKING TIME: 12 MINUTES

Chilli Bean Bonanza

SERVES 4–6	METRIC	IMPERIAL	AMERICAN
Onion, chopped	*1*	*1*	*1*
Garlic clove, crushed	*1*	*1*	*1*
Mushrooms, sliced	*100 g*	*4 oz*	*4 oz*
Small red (bell) pepper, chopped	*1*	*1*	*1*
Olive oil	*30 ml*	*2 tbsp*	*2 tbsp*
Can of chopped tomatoes	*400 g*	*14 oz*	*1 large*
Red chilli, seeded and chopped	*1*	*1*	*1*
Ground cumin	*5 ml*	*1 tsp*	*1 tsp*
Dried oregano	*5 ml*	*1 tsp*	*1 tsp*
Salt and freshly ground black pepper			
Cans of red kidney beans, drained	*2×425 g*	*2×15 oz*	*2 large*
Spaghetti	*350 g*	*12 oz*	*12 oz*
Grated Cheddar cheese, to serve			

1 Fry (sauté) the onion, garlic, mushrooms and pepper in the oil for 2 minutes, stirring.

2 Add the tomatoes, chilli, cumin, oregano and a little salt and pepper. Bring to the boil, reduce the heat and simmer for 10 minutes.

3 Stir in the beans and simmer for a further 5 minutes.

4 Meanwhile, cook the spaghetti according to the packet directions. Drain and pile on to warm plates.

5 Spoon the sauce over the spaghetti and serve with grated Cheddar cheese.

PREPARATION TIME: 10 MINUTES

COOKING TIME: 17 MINUTES

Spaghetti with Italian Mushrooms

SERVES 6	METRIC	IMPERIAL	AMERICAN
Onion, chopped	*1*	*1*	*1*
Olive oil	*90 ml*	*6 tbsp*	*6 tbsp*
White wine	*300 ml*	*½ pt*	*1¼ cups*
Salt and freshly ground black pepper			
Bouquet garni sachet	*1*	*1*	*1*
Garlic clove, finely chopped	*1*	*1*	*1*
Can of chopped tomatoes	*200 g*	*7 oz*	*1 small*
Button mushrooms, quartered	*350 g*	*12 oz*	*12 oz*
Black (mushroom) spaghetti	*350 g*	*12 oz*	*12 oz*
Chopped parsley, to garnish			

1 Fry (sauté) the onion in 60 ml/4 tbsp of the oil for 3 minutes until softened but not browned.

2 Add the remaining ingredients, except the pasta, bring to the boil, reduce the heat and simmer for about 15 minutes until the mushrooms are cooked and the liquid is reduced and thickened.

3 Remove the bouquet garni and adjust the seasoning.

4 Meanwhile, cook the pasta according to the packet directions. Drain, then toss in the remaining olive oil.

5 Spoon the mushroom sauce over the pasta and sprinkle with parsley before serving.

PREPARATION TIME: 5 MINUTES

COOKING TIME: 20 MINUTES

Chick Pea Goulash

Try adding diced green (bell) pepper, green beans or a diced courgette (zucchini) instead of peas.

SERVES 4	METRIC	IMPERIAL	AMERICAN
Onion, chopped	*1*	*1*	*1*
Garlic clove, crushed	*1*	*1*	*1*
Carrot, finely diced	*1*	*1*	*1*
Olive oil	*45 ml*	*3 tbsp*	*3 tbsp*
Paprika	*15 ml*	*1 tbsp*	*1 tbsp*
Can of chick peas (garbanzos)	*430 g*	*15½ oz*	*1 large*
Passata (sieved tomatoes)	*60 ml*	*4 tbsp*	*4 tbsp*
Tomato purée (paste)	*15 ml*	*1 tbsp*	*1 tbsp*
Dried mixed herbs	*2.5 ml*	*½ tsp*	*½ tsp*
Salt and freshly ground black pepper			
Frozen peas	*50 g*	*2 oz*	*2 oz*
Spaghetti	*350 g*	*12 oz*	*12 oz*
Soured (dairy sour) cream, caraway seeds and sesame seeds, to garnish			

1. Fry (sauté) the onion, garlic and carrot in the oil for 2 minutes until softened but not browned.
2. Add the paprika and fry for 1 minute, stirring.
3. Add the contents of the can of chick peas (including the liquid) and the remaining ingredients, except the pasta.
4. Bring to the boil, reduce the heat and simmer gently for about 10 minutes until thickened.
5. Meanwhile, cook the spaghetti according to the packet directions. Drain, then pile on to warm plates.

6 Spoon over the chick pea mixture. Top each portion with a spoonful of soured cream and a sprinkling of caraway and sesame seeds.

PREPARATION TIME: 5 MINUTES

COOKING TIME: 15 MINUTES

Rustic Aubergines with Red Kidney Beans

You can substitute other canned pulses for the red kidney beans.

SERVES 4	METRIC	IMPERIAL	AMERICAN
Small aubergine (eggplant), diced	*1*	*1*	*1*
Salt			
Olive oil	*45 ml*	*3 tbsp*	*3 tbsp*
Garlic clove, crushed	*1*	*1*	*1*
Can of red kidney beans, drained	*430 g*	*15½ oz*	*1 large*
Tomato purée (paste)	*30 ml*	*2 tbsp*	*2 tbsp*
Sun-dried tomato, chopped	*1*	*1*	*1*
Vegetable stock	*150 ml*	*¼ pt*	*⅔ cup*
Freshly ground black pepper			
Chopped basil	*15 ml*	*1 tbsp*	*1 tbsp*
Wholewheat spaghetti	*350 g*	*12 oz*	*12 oz*
Mascarpone cheese	*60 ml*	*4 tbsp*	*4 tbsp*
A few sprigs of basil, to garnish			

1 Sprinkle the aubergine with salt in a colander and leave to stand for 30 minutes. Rinse thoroughly in cold water and pat dry with kitchen paper.

2 Heat the oil in a saucepan, add the garlic and aubergine and fry (sauté), stirring, for 5 minutes.

3 Add the remaining ingredients, except the basil and spaghetti, bring to the boil, reduce the heat and simmer gently for 15 minutes until the sauce is reduced and slightly thickened.

4 Stir in the chopped basil.

5 Meanwhile, cook the spaghetti according to the packet directions. Drain and pile on to warm plates. Spoon the sauce over. Top with a spoonful of Mascarpone cheese and a sprig of basil.

PREPARATION TIME:
5 MINUTES
PLUS STANDING TIME

COOKING TIME:
20 MINUTES

Golden Pepper with Aubergine Tagliatelle

The yellow (bell) pepper makes an interesting colour combination with the aubergine (eggplant), although you can substitute a red or orange pepper instead.

SERVES 4	METRIC	IMPERIAL	AMERICAN
Large aubergine (eggplant), diced	*1*	*1*	*1*
Salt			
Olive oil	*60 ml*	*4 tbsp*	*4 tbsp*
Red onion, thinly sliced	*1*	*1*	*1*
Garlic clove, crushed	*1*	*1*	*1*
Yellow (bell) pepper, cut into thin strips	*1*	*1*	*1*
Ripe tomatoes, skinned, seeded and chopped	*2*	*2*	*2*
A few drops of anchovy essence (extract)			
Dried oregano	*2.5 ml*	*½ tsp*	*½ tsp*
Freshly ground black pepper			
Dry white wine	*150 ml*	*¼ pt*	*⅔ cup*
Egg tagliatelle	*350 g*	*12 oz*	*12 oz*
Olive oil and a few black olives, stoned (pitted), to garnish			

1 Place the aubergine in a colander, sprinkle with salt and leave to stand for 30 minutes. Drain, rinse with cold water and pat dry with kitchen paper.

2 Heat 45 ml/3 tbsp of the oil in a saucepan, add the aubergine and fry (sauté) until golden brown and tender, stirring. Remove from the pan and reserve.

3 Add the remaining oil and fry the onion and garlic for 2 minutes until slightly softened.

4 Add the pepper, tomatoes, anchovy essence, oregano and a good grinding of pepper. Return the aubergine to the pan, cover and simmer gently for 10 minutes or until pulpy, stirring occasionally.

5 Add the wine and simmer, uncovered, for about 5 minutes until well reduced. Taste and re-season, if necessary.

6 Meanwhile, cook the tagliatelle according to the packet directions. Drain and toss in a little olive oil.

7 Pile on to plates, spoon the sauce over and scatter with a few olives before serving.

PREPARATION TIME:
10 MINUTES
PLUS STANDING TIME

COOKING TIME:
20 MINUTES

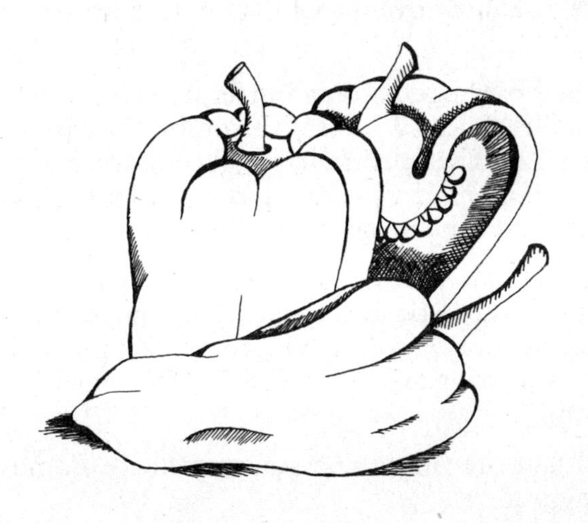

Mushroom Lasagne

SERVES 6	METRIC	IMPERIAL	AMERICAN
Unsalted (sweet) butter	*50 g*	*2 oz*	*¼ cup*
Onions, finely chopped	*2*	*2*	*2*
Assorted mushrooms (button, field, oyster, chanterelle, shiitake, etc.), sliced	*450 g*	*1 lb*	*1 lb*
Salt and freshly ground black pepper			
Chopped parsley	*30 ml*	*2 tbsp*	*2 tbsp*
Plain (all-purpose) flour	*25 g*	*1 oz*	*¼ cup*
Milk	*450 ml*	*¾ pt*	*2 cups*
Bay leaf	*1*	*1*	*1*
Sheets of no-need-to-precook lasagne	*8*	*8*	*8*
Parmesan cheese, freshly grated	*100 g*	*4 oz*	*1 cup*

1 Grease a shallow ovenproof dish with a little of the butter.

2 Heat half of the remaining butter in a large frying pan (skillet) and fry (sauté) the onion for 2 minutes, stirring. Add the mushrooms and cook for 5 minutes until tender and the juices are running. Season to taste and add the parsley.

3 Blend the flour well with a little of the milk in a saucepan, then stir in the remaining butter, milk and the bay leaf. Bring to the boil, then cook for 2 minutes, stirring all the time, until thickened and smooth.

4 Stir in half the cheese and season to taste. Remove the bay leaf.

5 Spoon a little of the cheese sauce into the base of the prepared dish. Top with a layer of lasagne sheets, breaking to fit, if necessary. Add a layer of mushrooms and their juice. Repeat the layers of lasagne and mushrooms, finishing with a layer of lasagne.

6 Spoon the remaining white sauce over and sprinkle with the remaining cheese.

7 Bake in a preheated oven at 190°C/375°F/gas mark 5 for about 35 minutes until cooked through and golden brown.

PREPARATION TIME:
10 MINUTES

COOKING TIME:
45 MINUTES

Devilled Mushroom Supper

SERVES 4	METRIC	IMPERIAL	AMERICAN
Twistetti	*225 g*	*8 oz*	*8 oz*
A knob of unsalted (sweet) butter			
Onion, finely chopped	*1*	*1*	*1*
Olive oil	*30 ml*	*2 tbsp*	*2 tbsp*
Button mushrooms, quartered	*350 g*	*12 oz*	*12 oz*
Tomatoes, skinned and chopped	*2*	*2*	*2*
Worcestershire sauce	*30 ml*	*2 tbsp*	*2 tbsp*
Tomato ketchup (catsup)	*30 ml*	*2 tbsp*	*2 tbsp*
A few drops of Tabasco sauce			
Wensleydale or Caerphilly cheese, crumbled, to serve	*75 g*	*3 oz*	*¾ cup*

1 Cook the twistetti according to the packet directions. Drain and toss in the butter. Spoon into a flameproof dish.

2 Meanwhile, fry (sauté) the onion in the oil for 2 minutes until softened but not browned.

3 Add the mushrooms and tomatoes and cook, stirring, for 2 minutes.

4 Add the remaining ingredients and cook gently for about 5 minutes until the mushrooms are cooked but not too soft.

5 Spoon over the pasta and sprinkle with crumbled Wensleydale or Caerphilly cheese. Flash under a hot grill (broiler) until the cheese bubbles.

PREPARATION TIME:
5 MINUTES

COOKING TIME:
13 MINUTES

Chanterelle Cream Ragu

SERVES 4	METRIC	IMPERIAL	AMERICAN
Streaky bacon, rinded and diced	*100 g*	*4 oz*	*4 oz*
Butter	*25 g*	*1 oz*	*2 tbsp*
Large onions, halved and sliced	*2*	*2*	*2*
Chanterelle mushrooms, halved	*450 g*	*1 lb*	*1 lb*
White wine	*150 ml*	*¼ pt*	*⅔ cup*
Chicken stock	*150 ml*	*¼ pt*	*⅔ cup*
Soy sauce	*30 ml*	*2 tbsp*	*2 tbsp*
Freshly ground black pepper			
Cornflour (cornstarch)	*15 ml*	*1 tbsp*	*1 tbsp*
Single (light) cream	*120 ml*	*4 fl oz*	*½ cup*
Fusilli	*350 g*	*12 oz*	*12 oz*
Chopped coriander (cilantro)	*30 ml*	*2 tbsp*	*2 tbsp*

1 Fry (sauté) the bacon in the butter for 2 minutes, stirring. Add the onion and cook, stirring, for 2 minutes until softened.

2 Add the chanterelles, wine, stock, soy sauce and a good grinding of pepper. Stir well, then bring to the boil. Reduce the heat and simmer for 10 minutes.

3 Blend the cornflour with the cream. Stir into the mixture, bring to the boil and cook, stirring, for 2 minutes.

4 Cook the fusilli according to the packet directions. Drain and pile on to plates. Spoon the sauce over and sprinkle with coriander.

PREPARATION TIME: 10 MINUTES

COOKING TIME: 17 MINUTES

Ratatouille Ruote

This ever-popular vegetable dish makes a perfect sauce for pasta.

SERVES 4–6	METRIC	IMPERIAL	AMERICAN
Olive oil	*45 ml*	*3 tbsp*	*3 tbsp*
Small aubergine (eggplant), diced	*1*	*1*	*1*
Courgettes (zucchini), sliced	*3*	*3*	*3*
Onion, chopped	*1*	*1*	*1*
Green (bell) pepper, diced	*1*	*1*	*1*
Tomatoes, chopped	*4*	*4*	*4*
Salt and freshly ground black pepper			
Tomato purée (paste)	*15 ml*	*1 tbsp*	*1 tbsp*
Red wine	*30 ml*	*2 tbsp*	*2 tbsp*
Chopped basil	*15 ml*	*1 tbsp*	*1 tbsp*
Ruote	*225 g*	*8 oz*	*8 oz*
Unsalted (sweet) butter	*15 g*	*½ oz*	*1 tbsp*
Freshly grated Parmesan cheese	*45 ml*	*3 tbsp*	*3 tbsp*
Grated Cheddar cheese	*45 ml*	*3 tbsp*	*3 tbsp*

1 Put the oil in a large saucepan. Add all the vegetables. Cook, stirring, for about 5 minutes until they are beginning to soften.

2 Add a little salt and pepper and the tomato purée, blended with the wine. Cover and simmer gently, stirring occasionally, for about 15 minutes until vegetables are tender but still have a little 'bite'. Stir in the basil just before serving.

3 Meanwhile, cook the ruote according to the packet directions. Drain, return to the pan and toss in the butter.

4 Layer in a flameproof dish with the ratatouille. Top with the cheeses and flash under a hot grill (broiler) until golden.

PREPARATION TIME: 10 MINUTES

COOKING TIME: 20 MINUTES

Quick Creamy Corn and Vegetable Pasta

You only need a few cans and a packet of dried pasta in the cupboard and you will always be able to make a nutritious and filling meal.

SERVES 4	METRIC	IMPERIAL	AMERICAN
Pasta, any shape	*225 g*	*8 oz*	*8 oz*
Can of creamed sweetcorn (corn)	*300 g*	*11 oz*	*1 large*
Can of mixed vegetables, drained	*200 g*	*7 oz*	*1 small*
Cheddar cheese, grated	*50 g*	*2 oz*	*½ cup*
Dried mixed herbs	*2.5 ml*	*½ tsp*	*½ tsp*
Freshly ground black pepper			
A little milk			
Crisp, fried (sautéed), crumbled bacon or chopped parsley, to garnish			
Extra grated Cheddar cheese, to serve			

1 Cook the pasta according to the packet directions. Drain and return to the pan.

2 Add the sweetcorn. Stir in the drained vegetables, cheese, herbs and a good grinding of pepper. Heat through, stirring all the time until piping hot.

3 Thin slightly with a little milk, if liked.

4 Pile into warm bowls, sprinkle with crisp crumbled bacon or chopped parsley. Serve with extra grated cheese handed separately.

PREPARATION TIME:
3 MINUTES

COOKING TIME:
10 MINUTES

Creamy Peas and Pasta Crécy-style

This sauce is also good made half with peas and half young broad beans.

SERVES 4	METRIC	IMPERIAL	AMERICAN
Tagliarini	*350 g*	*12 oz*	*12 oz*
Frozen peas	*225 g*	*8 oz*	*8 oz*
Sugar snap peas (optional)	*100 g*	*4 oz*	*4 oz*
Olive oil	*60 ml*	*4 tbsp*	*4 tbsp*
Bunch of watercress	*1*	*1*	*1*
Chopped basil leaves	*30 ml*	*2 tbsp*	*2 tbsp*
Crème fraîche	*120 ml*	*4 fl oz*	*½ cup*
Pinch of grated nutmeg	*1*	*1*	*1*
Salt and freshly ground black pepper			

1 Cook the tagliarini according to the packet directions. Drain.

2 Meanwhile, gently stew the peas and sugar snaps (if using) in the olive oil in a covered saucepan for 4 minutes, stirring occasionally. Don't have the heat too high or you will fry (sauté) rather than stew them.

3 Add the remaining ingredients with seasoning to taste, stir well and simmer for a further 2–3 minutes.

4 Add the cooked tagliarini, toss over a gentle heat and serve straight away.

PREPARATION TIME:
5 MINUTES

COOKING TIME:
10 MINUTES

Pappardelle with Green Asparagus Hollandaise

When asparagus is out of season, use canned or frozen spears. The texture and flavour won't be quite as good though. Reserve the asparagus trimmings and cooking liquid to make soup.

SERVES 4	METRIC	IMPERIAL	AMERICAN
Asparagus	*450 g*	*1 lb*	*1 lb*
Pappardelle	*350 g*	*12 oz*	*12 oz*
Bunch of watercress	*1*	*1*	*1*
Chopped parsley	*30 ml*	*2 tbsp*	*2 tbsp*
Eggs	*2*	*2*	*2*
Lemon juice	*30 ml*	*2 tbsp*	*2 tbsp*
Unsalted (sweet) butter, melted	*150 g*	*5 oz*	*⅔ cup*
Caster (superfine) sugar	*1.5 ml*	*¼ tsp*	*¼ tsp*
Salt and white pepper			
Cayenne, to garnish			

1 Trim the asparagus stalks and tie the spears in a bundle.

2 Stand the bundle in a pan of boiling, lightly salted water. Cover with a lid or foil and simmer for 10 minutes. Turn off the heat and leave for about 5 minutes. Drain. Cut the spears into short lengths. Keep warm.

3 Meanwhile, cook the pasta according to the packet directions. Drain and return to the pan.

4 Trim off the watercress stalks and chop the leaves. Mix with the parsley.

5 Whisk the eggs in a saucepan with the lemon juice. Gradually whisk in 100 g/4 oz/½ cup of the melted butter. Cook, whisking all the time, over a gentle heat until thickened. Do not allow to boil or the mixture will curdle.

6 Add the sugar and season to taste.

7 Add the remaining butter to the pasta with the asparagus and toss gently. Soon on to warm plates and drizzle the Hollandaise sauce over. Sprinkle with cayenne and serve.

PREPARATION TIME: 15 MINUTES

COOKING TIME: 20 MINUTES

Mediterranean Courgette Lasagne

This is equally good made with diced marrow (squash) instead of courgettes (zucchini).

SERVES 4	METRIC	IMPERIAL	AMERICAN
Olive oil	*60 ml*	*4 tbsp*	*4 tbsp*
Onion, chopped	*1*	*1*	*1*
Garlic clove, crushed	*1*	*1*	*1*
Courgettes (zucchini), sliced	*6*	*6*	*6*
Ripe tomatoes, skinned, seeded and chopped	*4*	*4*	*4*
Tomato purée (paste)	*15 ml*	*1 tbsp*	*1 tbsp*
Caster (superfine) sugar	*5 ml*	*1 tsp*	*1 tsp*
Salt and freshly ground black pepper			
Black olives, stoned (pitted)	*12*	*12*	*12*
Sheets of no-need-to-precook lasagne	*8*	*8*	*8*
Crème fraîche	*150 ml*	*¼ pt*	*⅔ cup*
Eggs	*2*	*2*	*2*
Parmesan cheese, freshly grated	*50 g*	*2 oz*	*½ cup*

1 Heat the oil in a large saucepan. Add the onion and fry (sauté) for 2 minutes until softened but not browned.

2 Add the garlic, courgettes and tomatoes and cook, stirring, for 3 minutes until the courgettes are slightly softened.

3 Add the tomato purée, sugar, a little salt and pepper and the olives. Cover and simmer gently for about 15 minutes.

4 Layer with the lasagne in a large, shallow ovenproof dish, ending with a layer of lasagne.

5 Beat the remaining ingredients together and pour over. Bake in a preheated oven at 190°C/375°F/ gas mark 5 for 40 minutes until cooked through and golden brown on top.

PREPARATION TIME: 10 MINUTES

COOKING TIME: 1 HOUR

Crunchy Cauliflower with Coriander Tagliatelle

The courgettes (zucchini) are added for colour. Use peas or green beans instead, if preferred.

SERVES 4	METRIC	IMPERIAL	AMERICAN
Green (spinach) tagliatelle	*350 g*	*12 oz*	*12 oz*
Butter	*75 g*	*3 oz*	*⅓ cup*
Thick slices of bread, cubed	*2*	*2*	*2*
Onion, chopped	*1*	*1*	*1*
Garlic clove, crushed	*1*	*1*	*1*
Ground cumin	*5 ml*	*1 tsp*	*1 tsp*
Courgettes (zucchini) diced	*2*	*2*	*2*
Small cauliflower, cut into tiny florets	*1*	*1*	*1*
Double (heavy) cream	*150 ml*	*¼ pt*	*⅔ cup*
Chopped coriander (cilantro)	*15 ml*	*1 tbsp*	*1 tbsp*
Salt and freshly ground black pepper			
A few sprigs of coriander, to garnish			

1 Cook the tagliatelle according to the packet directions. Drain.

2 Melt 50 g/2 oz/¼ cup of the butter in a frying pan (skillet) and fry (sauté) the bread cubes until crisp and golden. Drain on kitchen paper.

3 Melt the remaining butter in a saucepan, add the onion and garlic and fry gently for 2 minutes. Add the cumin and fry for 1 minute.

4 Add the courgettes, stir gently, then cover, reduce the heat and simmer for 5 minutes until the courgettes are just tender.

5 Meanwhile, cook the cauliflower florets in boiling salted water for 4–5 minutes until just tender. Drain.

6 Add the cauliflower to the courgette mixture. Stir in the cream, coriander and seasoning.

7 Add the cooked tagliatelle and toss over a gentle heat until piping hot.

8 Spoon on to warm plates, sprinkle with the croûtons and garnish with sprigs of coriander.

PREPARATION TIME: 10 MINUTES

COOKING TIME: 12 MINUTES

Tagliatelle alla Salsa di Pomodoro

This classic sauce can be tarted up with herbs, ham, bacon or pancetta, peppers, mushrooms, tuna – you name it!

SERVES 4	METRIC	IMPERIAL	AMERICAN
Olive oil	*15 ml*	*1 tbsp*	*1 tbsp*
Large onion, finely chopped	*1*	*1*	*1*
Garlic cloves, crushed	*2*	*2*	*2*
Large, ripe tomatoes, skinned and chopped	*8*	*8*	*8*
Salt and freshly ground black pepper			
Tagliatelle	*350 g*	*12 oz*	*12 oz*
Unsalted (sweet) butter	*15 g*	*½ oz*	*1 tbsp*
Fresh Parmesan cheese, shaved into flakes with a potato peeler, to garnish			

1 Heat the oil in a saucepan and add the onion and garlic. Fry (sauté), stirring, for about 4 minutes, until soft and lightly golden.

2 Reduce the heat and add the tomatoes. Simmer for 10 minutes until pulpy, stirring occasionally. Season well with a little salt and lots of pepper.

3 Meanwhile, cook the tagliatelle according to the packet directions. Drain and return to the pan. Add the butter and toss until coated.

4 Pile on to warm plates and spoon the tomato sauce over. Top with flakes of Parmesan and serve hot.

PREPARATION TIME: 10 MINUTES

COOKING TIME: 14 MINUTES

Roast Vegetable Fettucci

SERVESS 4	METRIC	IMPERIAL	AMERICAN
Courgettes (zucchini), cut into chunks	*2*	*2*	*2*
Red onion, quartered	*1*	*1*	*1*
Small aubergine (eggplant), cut into chunks	*1*	*1*	*1*
Yellow, red and green (bell) peppers, quartered	*1 of each*	*1 of each*	*1 of each*
Olive oil			
Dried oregano	*5 ml*	*1 tsp*	*1 tsp*
Salt and freshly ground black pepper			
Fettucci	*350 g*	*12 oz*	*12 oz*
Mozzarella cheese, sliced	*225 g*	*8 oz*	*8 oz*
A few basil leaves, chopped, to garnish			

1. Put the prepared vegetables in a roasting tin (pan).
2. Drizzle with olive oil and sprinkle with the oregano and a little salt and pepper.
3. Roast in the oven at 190°C/375°F/gas mark 5 for about 30 minutes, stirring once or twice, until turning golden brown on top.
4. Meanwhile, cook the fettucci according to the packet directions. Drain and place in a flameproof dish.
5. Spoon the vegetables and the juices over. Top with the Mozzarella, grill (broil) until the cheese bubbles and sprinkle with chopped basil. Serve straight away.

PREPARATION TIME:
10 MINUTES

COOKING TIME:
30 MINUTES

Spaghetti with Spiced Carrot and Garlic Purée

A watercress, orange and tomato salad makes a delicious accompaniment to this dish.

SERVES 4	METRIC	IMPERIAL	AMERICAN
Carrots, chopped	*750 g*	*1½ lb*	*1½ lb*
Milk	*30 ml*	*2 tbsp*	*2 tbsp*
Butter	*50 g*	*2 oz*	*¼ cup*
Garlic clove, crushed	*1*	*1*	*1*
Mixed (apple-pie) spice	*1.5 ml*	*¼ tsp*	*¼ tsp*
Salt and freshly ground black pepper			
Black (mushroom) or egg spaghetti	*350 g*	*12 oz*	*12 oz*
Chopped parsley and crumbled Feta cheese, to garnish			

1 Put the carrots in a saucepan with just enough water to cover them. Bring to the boil and cook for about 10 minutes until really tender. Drain, but reserve the cooking liquid.

2 Turn the carrots into a food processor or blender with the milk, 40 g/1½ oz/3 tbsp of the butter and the garlic. Run the machine until the mixture is smooth.

3 Return to the saucepan. Add the mixed spice, salt and pepper to taste and enough of the cooking water to give a smooth purée. Heat through gently until piping hot.

4 Meanwhile, cook the spaghetti according to the packet directions. Drain and toss in the remaining butter.

5 Pile on to warm plates. Spoon the sauce over. Sprinkle with parsley and crumbled Feta cheese before serving.

PREPARATION TIME: 15 MINUTES

COOKING TIME: 12 MINUTES

Green Goddess

When fresh spinach is unavailable, use 225 g/8 oz frozen spinach, thawed and well squeezed out.

SERVES 4	METRIC	IMPERIAL	AMERICAN
Can of anchovy fillets	*50 g*	*2 oz*	*1 small*
Milk	*45 ml*	*3 tbsp*	*3 tbsp*
Spinach	*450 g*	*1 lb*	*1 lb*
Bunch of spring onions (scallions), chopped	*1*	*1*	*1*
Olive oil	*45 ml*	*3 tbsp*	*3 tbsp*
Butter	*25 g*	*1 oz*	*2 tbsp*
Vegetable stock	*150 ml*	*¼ pt*	*⅔ cup*
Grated nutmeg	*1.5 ml*	*¼ tsp*	*¼ tsp*
Crème fraîche	*30 ml*	*2 tbsp*	*2 tbsp*
Freshly ground black pepper			
Spaghetti	*350 g*	*12 oz*	*12 oz*
Parma ham or thinly sliced Milano salami, cut into narrow strips, to garnish			
Grated Pecorino cheese, to serve			

1 Soak the anchovies in milk for 5 minutes, drain and chop.

2 Wash the spinach well under running water. Place in a saucepan with any water adhering to the leaves. Cover and cook gently for 4–5 minutes until really tender. Drain well, then squeeze out any remaining moisture.

3 Fry (sauté) the spring onions in the oil and butter for 5 minutes until soft. Add the anchovies and spinach and cook for 1 further minute.

4 Place in a blender or processor. Add the stock and run the machine until the mixture is smooth. Stir in the nutmeg and crème fraîche and season to taste with pepper.

5 Return to the saucepan and heat through, stirring, until piping hot.

6 Meanwhile, cook the spaghetti according to the packet directions. Drain. Pile on to warm plates.

7 Spoon the sauce over and top with strips of Parma ham or Milano salami. Serve with Pecorino cheese.

PREPARATION TIME: 10 MINUTES

COOKING TIME: 15 MINUTES

Cheesy Leek Supper

For extra colour and flavour, try adding a diced green or red (bell) pepper when cooking the leeks.

SERVES 4	METRIC	IMPERIAL	AMERICAN
Leeks, sliced	*3*	*3*	*3*
Butter	*50 g*	*2 oz*	*¼ cup*
Plain (all-purpose) flour	*20 g*	*¾ oz*	*3 tbsp*
Milk	*300 ml*	*½ pt*	*1¼ cups*
Dijon mustard	*5 ml*	*1 tsp*	*1 tsp*
Cheddar cheese, grated	*150 g*	*5 oz*	*1¼ cups*
Salt and freshly ground black pepper			
Short-cut macaroni	*225 g*	*8 oz*	*8 oz*
Chopped parsley, to garnish			

1 Fry (sauté) the leeks in the butter for 2 minutes until they begin to soften. Reduce the heat, cover and cook gently for 10 minutes until tender.

2 Stir in the flour and cook for 1 minute. Gradually blend in the milk. Bring to the boil and simmer for 2 minutes, stirring.

3 Stir in the mustard, half the cheese and salt and pepper to taste.

4 Meanwhile, cook the macaroni according to the packet directions. Drain.

5 Add to the sauce. Toss well and turn into a flameproof dish. Sprinkle with the remaining cheese and brown under a hot grill (broiler).

PREPARATION TIME:
5 MINUTES

COOKING TIME:
15 MINUTES

CHEESE, EGG & CREAM DISHES

All types of cheese, cream and eggs blend beautifully with pasta to give highly nutritious, delicious meals. For perfect results, don't cook for too long after adding eggs or cheese. You are looking for velvety, creamy results, not rubbery strings, scrambles or curdles! These dishes are quite rich and are best served with a crisp mixed leaf salad and some warm crusty bread – perhaps ciabatta flavoured with olives, mushrooms or sun-dried tomatoes.

Macaroni Cheese

SERVES 4	METRIC	IMPERIAL	AMERICAN
Short-cut macaroni	*175 g*	*6 oz*	*6 oz*
Plain (all-purpose) flour	*20 g*	*¾ oz*	*3 tbsp*
Milk	*300 ml*	*½ pt*	*1¼ cups*
Butter or margarine	*20 g*	*¾ oz*	*1½ tbsp*
Made English mustard	*2.5 ml*	*½ tsp*	*½ tsp*
Cheddar cheese, grated	*100 g*	*4 oz*	*1 cup*
Salt and freshly ground black pepper			
Cornflakes	*45 ml*	*3 tbsp*	*3 tbsp*
Tomatoes, sliced	*2*	*2*	*2*

1 Cook the macaroni according to the packet directions. Drain.

2 Put the flour in a saucepan and whisk in the milk. Add the butter, bring to the boil and cook for 2 minutes, stirring.

3 Stir in the mustard and three-quarters of the cheese and season to taste.

4 Mix in the macaroni and place in a flameproof dish.

5 Mix the crushed cornflakes with the remaining cheese and scatter over the top. Arrange the sliced tomatoes around the edge.

6 Place under a preheated grill (broiler) until golden and bubbling. Serve hot.

PREPARATION TIME:
10 MINUTES

COOKING TIME:
15 MINUTES

Variations

Macaroni and Tomato Cheese
Prepare as for Macaroni Cheese (page 118) but put half the macaroni cheese mixture in the dish. Top with a layer of 225 g/8 oz/1 small can of chopped tomatoes, sprinkle with dried or chopped basil, then add the remaining macaroni cheese. Continue as before.

Macaroni and Sweetcorn Cheese
Prepare as for Macaroni and Tomato Cheese (above), but put 200 g/7 oz/1 small can sweetcorn (corn), drained, in the middle instead of the tomatoes.

Macaroni and Spinach Cheese
Prepare as for Macaroni and Tomato Cheese (above), but put 295 g/10½ oz/1 small can spinach, drained, in a layer instead of the tomatoes.

Macaroni and Mushroom Cheese
Prepare as for Macaroni Cheese (page 118), but mix 295 g/10½ oz/1 small can sliced mushrooms, drained, in with the macaroni before turning into the dish.

Macaroni and Tuna Cheese
Prepare as for Macaroni Cheese (page 118), but stir 185 g/6½ oz/1 small can drained tuna into the macaroni mixture and flavour with 1.5 ml/¼ tsp dried mixed herbs before turning into the dish.

Ricotta Cheese and Broccoli Tagliatelle

Asparagus spears cut into small pieces make a delicious alternative to the broccoli.

SERVES 4	METRIC	IMPERIAL	AMERICAN
Green (spinach) tagliatelle	*350 g*	*12 oz*	*12 oz*
Broccoli, cut into tiny florets	*450 g*	*1 lb*	*1 lb*
Butter, melted	*90 g*	*3½ oz*	*scant ½ cup*
Ricotta cheese	*175 g*	*6 oz*	*¾ cup*
Parmesan cheese, freshly grated	*50 g*	*2 oz*	*½ cup*
Chopped parsley	*60 ml*	*4 tbsp*	*4 tbsp*
Cayenne	*1.5 ml*	*¼ tsp*	*¼ tsp*
Salt and freshly ground black pepper			
Poppy seeds	*1.5 ml*	*1 tbsp*	*1 tbsp*
Fennel seeds	*1.5 ml*	*1 tbsp*	*1 tbsp*
Sesame seeds, toasted	*1.5 ml*	*1 tbsp*	*1 tbsp*

1 Cook the pasta according to the packet directions and add the broccoli for the last 4 minutes' cooking time. Drain and return to the pan.

2 Add the butter, the cheeses and parsley and heat through, tossing gently. Season to taste with salt and pepper.

3 Pile on to plates. Mix the seeds together and sprinkle over.

PREPARATION TIME:
5 MINUTES

COOKING TIME:
12 MINUTES

Cheese Pasta with Breadcrumb Crunch

Use cider or white wine instead of beer, if you prefer.

SERVES 4	METRIC	IMPERIAL	AMERICAN
Conchiglie	*225 g*	*8 oz*	*8 oz*
Cheddar cheese, grated	*350 g*	*12 oz*	*3 cups*
Made mustard	*10 ml*	*2 tsp*	*2 tsp*
Light ale	*60 ml*	*4 tbsp*	*4 tbsp*
A little milk			
Fresh breadcrumbs	*60 ml*	*4 tbsp*	*4 tbsp*
Butter	*15 g*	*½ oz*	*1 tbsp*
Snipped chives, to garnish			

1. Cook the pasta according to the packet directions. Drain.
2. Put the remaining ingredients in a saucepan and heat through until the cheese has melted and the mixture is well blended. Add a little milk if the mixture seems too sticky.
3. Add the pasta and toss well. Sprinkle liberally with chives and fried buttered breadcrumbs before serving.
4. Meanwhile, fry (sauté) the breadcrumbs in the butter until golden, adding a little more butter, if necessary.
5. Pile the pasta on to warm plates, top with the breadcrumbs and serve garnished liberally with snipped chives.

PREPARATION TIME: 5 MINUTES

COOKING TIME: 10 MINUTES

Dolcelatte Dream

Try using other soft blue cheeses for variety.

SERVES 4	METRIC	IMPERIAL	AMERICAN
Multi-coloured tagliatelle	*350 g*	*12 oz*	*12 oz*
Celery sticks, finely chopped	*2*	*2*	*2*
Butter	*25 g*	*1 oz*	*2 tbsp*
Dolcelatte, diced	*100 g*	*4 oz*	*4 oz*
Medium-fat soft cheese	*50 g*	*2 oz*	*¼ cup*
Single (light) cream	*90 ml*	*6 tbsp*	*6 tbsp*
Chopped parsley	*15 ml*	*1 tbsp*	*1 tbsp*
Freshly ground black pepper			

1 Cook the pasta according to the packet directions. Drain.

2 Meanwhile, put the celery and butter in a double saucepan or in a bowl over a pan of gently simmering water. Cover and cook gently for about 8 minutes or until softened.

3 Add the cheeses and cook, stirring, until smooth and melted.

4 Stir in the cream and parsley. Add plenty of pepper and stir well.

5 Add the cooked tagliatelle, toss well and serve piping hot.

PREPARATION TIME:
3 MINUTES

COOKING TIME:
12 MINUTES

Garlic and Herb Tortellini

This is particularly good served as a starter or as a side dish with grilled meat, poultry or fish.

SERVES 4–6	METRIC	IMPERIAL	AMERICAN
Cheese-stuffed tortellini	*225 g*	*8 oz*	*8 oz*
Cornflour (cornstarch)	*15 ml*	*1 tbsp*	*1 tbsp*
Milk	*300 ml*	*½ pt*	*1¼ cups*
Butter	*15 g*	*½ oz*	*1 tbsp*
Garlic and herb cheese	*90 g*	*3½ oz*	*scant ½ cup*

Salt and freshly ground black pepper

Snipped chives, to garnish

1 Cook the tortellini according to the packet directions. Drain.

2 Meanwhile, whisk the cornflour with a little of the milk in a saucepan. Stir in the remaining milk and add the butter.

3 Bring to the boil, stirring until thickened.

4 Add the cheese and stir over a gentle heat until smooth. Season with salt and pepper. Stir in the tortellini.

5 Pile on to warm plates and sprinkle with snipped chives before serving.

PREPARATION TIME: 3 MINUTES

COOKING TIME: 15 MINUTES

Goatherd's Mountain Special

The crumbled goats' cheese is added just before serving so it just begins to melt as it is served.

SERVES 4–6	METRIC	IMPERIAL	AMERICAN
Spaghettini	*350 g*	*12 oz*	*12 oz*
Olive oil	*120 ml*	*4 fl oz*	*½ cup*
Garlic cloves, crushed	*2*	*2*	*2*
Ripe tomatoes, diced	*4*	*4*	*4*
Salt and freshly ground black pepper			
Basil leaves, torn	*16*	*16*	*16*
Goats' cheese, roughly crumbled	*50 g*	*2 oz*	*½ cup*
A few black olives, stoned (pitted), to garnish (optional)			

1 Cook the spaghettini according to the packet directions. Drain.

2 Heat the oil in the same saucepan. Add the garlic and cook gently for 1 minute.

3 Add the tomatoes and a little salt and pepper and cook gently for 1–2 minutes, stirring until heated through but with the tomatoes still in pieces.

4 Add the pasta, basil leaves and cheese and toss gently.

5 Pile on to plates and serve immediately, garnished with a few black olives, if liked.

PREPARATION TIME: 5 MINUTES

COOKING TIME: 10 MINUTES

Farfalle with Goats' Cheese, Radicchio and Peppercorns

This is good served with a tomato and onion salad.

SERVES 4	METRIC	IMPERIAL	AMERICAN
Wholewheat farfalle	*225 g*	*8 oz*	*8 oz*
Butter	*25 g*	*1 oz*	*2 tbsp*
Garlic cloves, finely chopped	*2*	*2*	*2*
Head of radicchio, coarsely shredded	*1*	*1*	*1*
Salt			
Pickled green peppercorns	*5 ml*	*1 tsp*	*1 tsp*
Double (heavy) cream	*250 ml*	*8 fl oz*	*1 cup*
Goats' cheese, crumbled	*50 g*	*2 oz*	*½ cup*
Freshly ground black or green pepper, to garnish			

1 Cook the farfalle according to the packet directions. Drain.

2 Meanwhile, melt the butter in a saucepan. Add the garlic and radicchio, toss, then cover and cook gently for 4 minutes.

3 Season lightly with salt and add the peppercorns.

4 In a separate pan, heat the cream. Add half the cheese and whisk until smooth.

5 Stir in the radicchio mixture.

6 Add the remaining cheese to the cooked farfalle. Toss quickly and pile on to warm serving plates. Spoon the sauce over and add a good grinding of pepper.

PREPARATION TIME:
5 MINUTES

COOKING TIME:
10 MINUTES

Nutty Gorgonzola

This is very rich, so serve in small portions with a crisp salad and some crusty bread.

SERVES 6	METRIC	IMPERIAL	AMERICAN
Wholewheat rotelli	*225 g*	*8 oz*	*8 oz*
Garlic cloves, finely chopped	*2*	*2*	*2*
Butter	*25 g*	*1 oz*	*2 tbsp*
Gorgonzola, crumbled	*225 g*	*8 oz*	*2 cups*
Walnuts, chopped	*50 g*	*2 oz*	*½ cup*
Salt and freshly ground black pepper			
Milk or single (light) cream	*30 ml*	*2 tbsp*	*2 tbsp*
Freshly grated Parmesan cheese	*30 ml*	*2 tbsp*	*2 tbsp*
Chopped parsley, to garnish			

1 Cook the pasta according to the packet directions. Drain.

2 Melt the butter in the same pan and cook the garlic gently for 1 minute.

3 Add the remaining ingredients and heat through gently until the cheese is melted and well combined. Do not allow to boil. Add the cooked rotelli. Toss and serve garnished with parsley.

PREPARATION TIME: 5 MINUTES

COOKING TIME: 12 MINUTES

Fresh Parmesan with Avocado Tortellini

SERVES 4	METRIC	IMPERIAL	AMERICAN
Mushroom-stuffed tortellini	*225 g*	*8 oz*	*8 oz*
Double (heavy) cream	*175 ml*	*6 fl oz*	*¾ cup*
Ripe avocado, peeled and stoned (pitted)	*1*	*1*	*1*
Parmesan cheese, freshly grated	*75 g*	*3 oz*	*¾ cup*
Lemon juice	*30 ml*	*2 tbsp*	*2 tbsp*
Salt and freshly ground black pepper			
Tiny sprigs of watercress, to garnish			

1 Cook the tortellini according to the packet directions. Drain.

2 Place the cream in a saucepan and heat gently but do not boil.

3 Meanwhile, purée the avocado in a blender or food processor with the cheese and lemon juice. Alternatively, mash well with a fork, then beat until smooth.

4 Stir into the hot cream and season well. Add the cooked tortellini, toss until hot through and serve straight away with a few tiny sprigs of watercress scattered over.

PREPARATION TIME: 5 MINUTES

COOKING TIME: 15 MINUTES

Spaghetti alla Cipriota

This is a glorious mixture of salty and sweet flavours. It makes a delicious summer lunch dish. Once cooked, serve immediately before the cheese melts completely.

SERVES 4	METRIC	IMPERIAL	AMERICAN
Spaghetti	*350 g*	*12 oz*	*12 oz*
Olive oil	*60 ml*	*4 tbsp*	*4 tbsp*
Garlic cloves, chopped	*2*	*2*	*2*
Spring onions (scallions), chopped	*4*	*4*	*4*
Dried oregano	*5 ml*	*1 tsp*	*1 tsp*
Large beefsteak tomato, diced	*1*	*1*	*1*
Freshly ground black pepper			
Black Greek olives, stoned (pitted)	*75 g*	*3 oz*	*½ cup*
Freshly grated Parmesan cheese	*30 ml*	*2 tbsp*	*2 tbsp*
Chilled Feta cheese, crumbled	*100 g*	*4 oz*	*1 cup*
Roughly chopped mint	*30 ml*	*2 tbsp*	*2 tbsp*
A little extra olive oil and freshly grated Parmesan cheese, to serve			

1. Cook the spaghetti according to the packet directions. Drain.
2. Heat the oil in the same saucepan. Add the garlic and spring onions and soften for 1 minute.
3. Add the oregano, tomato and a good grinding of pepper and cook gently for 1–2 minutes until hot but the tomato pieces still hold their shape.
4. Add the remaining ingredients and the spaghetti and toss lightly over a gentle heat to combine.

5 Pile on to warm plates, drizzle with a little extra olive oil and sprinkle with Parmesan before serving.

PREPARATION TIME: 5 MINUTES

COOKING TIME: 15 MINUTES

Tagliatelle ai Quattro Formaggi

SERVES 4	METRIC	IMPERIAL	AMERICAN
Green (spinach) tagliatelle	*350 g*	*12 oz*	*12 oz*
Emmental (Swiss) cheese, grated	*100 g*	*4 oz*	*1 cup*
Fontina cheese, grated	*100 g*	*4 oz*	*1 cup*
Gouda cheese, grated	*100 g*	*4 oz*	*1 cup*
Parmesan cheese, freshly grated	*100 g*	*4 oz*	*1 cup*
Unsalted (sweet) butter	*100 g*	*4 oz*	*1 cup*
Salt and freshly ground black pepper			
A few torn basil leaves, to garnish			

1 Cook the pasta according to the packet directions. Drain and return to the pan.

2 Add the cheeses, the butter in small flakes, a little salt and a good grinding of pepper.

3 Toss over a gentle heat until the cheese has just melted, then pile on to plates and serve immediately, garnished with a few torn basil leaves.

PREPARATION TIME: 15 MINUTES

COOKING TIME: 12 MINUTES

Tocco di Noci

SERVES 4	METRIC	IMPERIAL	AMERICAN
Tagliatelle	*350 g*	*12 oz*	*12 oz*
Shelled walnuts	*225 g*	*8 oz*	*8 oz*
Thick slice of white bread, crusts removed	*1*	*1*	*1*
Milk	*75 ml*	*5 tbsp*	*5 tbsp*
Garlic clove, crushed	*1*	*1*	*1*
Salt and freshly ground black pepper			
Olive oil	*45 ml*	*3 tbsp*	*3 tbsp*
Mascarpone cheese	*100 g*	*4 oz*	*½ cup*

1 Cook the tagliatelle according to the packet directions. Drain and return to the pan.

2 Meanwhile, place the nuts in boiling water for 2 minutes. Drain and rub off the skins in a clean tea towel (dish cloth).

3 Soak the bread in the milk.

4 Grind the nuts to a fine powder in a food processor.

5 Squeeze out the bread and add to the nuts with the garlic and a little salt and pepper. Run the machine until the mixture is smooth.

6 With the machine running, add the oil in a thin stream and then finally add the cheese.

7 Add to the freshly cooked tagliatelle and toss over a gentle heat until hot through. Serve immediately.

PREPARATION TIME:
10–15 MINUTES

COOKING TIME:
12 MINUTES

Creamy Jalapeno Pepper Fettuccine

Serve this with an avocado and cucumber salad.

SERVES 4–6	METRIC	IMPERIAL	AMERICAN
White wine vinegar	*120 ml*	*4 fl oz*	*½ cup*
Salt	*2.5 ml*	*½ tsp*	*½ tsp*
Small onion, finely chopped	*1*	*1*	*1*
Jalapeno pepper, seeded and chopped	*1*	*1*	*1*
Double (heavy) cream	*600 ml*	*1 pt*	*2½ cups*
Chopped coriander (cilantro)	*30 ml*	*2 tbsp*	*2 tbsp*
Fettuccine	*350 g*	*12 oz*	*12 oz*

1 Put the vinegar, salt, onion and chilli in a saucepan. Bring to the boil and boil rapidly for about 5 minutes until the mixture is reduced by half.

2 Add the cream, bring to the boil and boil rapidly until the mixture is well reduced and thickened – about 15 minutes.

3 Add half the coriander and stir well.

4 Meanwhile, cook the fettuccine according to the packet directions. Drain and return to the pan.

5 Add the sauce, toss over a gentle heat, then serve sprinkled with the remaining coriander.

PREPARATION TIME:
5 MINUTES

COOKING TIME:
20 MINUTES

Pasta Con Salsa Alfredo

This is one of the simplest ways of serving good fresh pasta – ideal if you've bothered to make your own.

SERVES 4	METRIC	IMPERIAL	AMERICAN
Fresh pasta, bought or home-made (see page 156)	*450 g*	*1 lb*	*1 lb*
Double (heavy) cream	*450 ml*	*¾ pt*	*2 cups*
Butter	*50 g*	*2 oz*	*¼ cup*
Parmesan cheese, freshly grated	*175 g*	*6 oz*	*1½ cups*
Freshly ground black pepper			
Crisp, fried (sautéed), crumbled bacon (optional), to garnish			

1. Bring the cream and butter to the boil in a saucepan. Reduce the heat and simmer for 1 minute.
2. Add half the cheese and some pepper and whisk until smooth.
3. Meanwhile, cook the pasta in plenty of boiling salted water for 4 minutes. Drain.
4. Add the pasta and the rest of the cheese to the sauce and toss well over a gentle heat. Pile on to warm plates and sprinkle with a good grinding of black pepper and crisp crumbled bacon, if liked.

PREPARATION TIME: 3 MINUTES

COOKING TIME: 4 MINUTES

Spaghetti alla Carbonara

This sauce is also very good with the addition of 50 g/2 oz sliced button mushrooms.

SERVES 4	METRIC	IMPERIAL	AMERICAN
Spaghetti	*350 g*	*12 oz*	*12 oz*
Unsmoked streaky bacon, cut into small dice	*100 g*	*4 oz*	*4 oz*
Butter	*75 g*	*3 oz*	*⅓ cup*
Eggs	*5*	*5*	*5*
Chopped parsley	*30 ml*	*2 tbsp*	*2 tbsp*
Salt and freshly ground black pepper			
Parmesan cheese, freshly grated	*50 g*	*2 oz*	*½ cup*

1 Cook the spaghetti according to the packet directions. Drain and return to the pan.

2 Meanwhile, fry (sauté) the bacon in the butter until browned.

3 Beat the eggs with the parsley, a little salt and lots of pepper and the cheese.

4 Add the bacon mixture and the egg mixture to the spaghetti and toss quickly until the spaghetti is coated but do not let it scramble. The mixture should be creamy and hot. Serve straight away.

PREPARATION TIME:
5 MINUTES

COOKING TIME:
10 MINUTES

Mafalde con Salsa alla Panna

For a more exotic version, use pancetta or a raw cured ham such as Parma instead of cooked ham.

SERVES 4	METRIC	IMPERIAL	AMERICAN
Mafalde	*350 g*	*12 oz*	*12 oz*
Butter	*40 g*	*1½ oz*	*3 tbsp*
Cooked sliced ham, cut into tiny strips	*100 g*	*4 oz*	*4 oz*
Double (heavy) cream	*75 ml*	*5 tbsp*	*5 tbsp*
Salt and freshly ground black pepper			
Freshly grated nutmeg			
Freshly grated Parmesan cheese, to garnish			

1. Cook the mafalde according to the packet directions. Drain.
2. Melt the butter in the same saucepan. Add the cream, ham, a sprinkling of salt, a good grinding of pepper and lots of grated nutmeg and heat through for 1 minute.
3. Add the cooked mafalde and toss over a gentle heat for 2 minutes. Serve garnished with lots of freshly grated Parmesan cheese.

PREPARATION TIME: 5 MINUTES

COOKING TIME: 14 MINUTES

Scrambled Egg and Smoked Salmon Mafalde

The trick is to only half-scramble the eggs before adding the pasta so every strand gets bathed in sauce.

SERVES 4–6	METRIC	IMPERIAL	AMERICAN
Mafalde	*350 g*	*12 oz*	*12 oz*
Butter	*15 g*	*½ oz*	*1 tbsp*
Eggs, beaten	*4*	*4*	*4*
Single (light) cream	*150 ml*	*¼ pt*	*⅔ cup*
Smoked salmon pieces, cut into tiny strips	*100 g*	*4 oz*	*4 oz*
Freshly ground black pepper			
Chopped parsley, to garnish			

1 Cook the mafalde according to the packet directions. Drain.

2 Melt the butter in the same saucepan. Add the eggs and cream and whisk lightly.

3 Stir over a gentle heat until half-scrambled but still quite runny. Stir in the pasta and salmon and a good grinding of black pepper. Toss lightly over a gentle heat until the mixture is just scrambled but still creamy. Serve straight away garnished with chopped parsley.

PREPARATION TIME:
5 MINUTES

COOKING TIME:
15–20 MINUTES

SALADS

Tempting, cool, exotic and easy-to-eat are all words that describe pasta salads. They are perfect for picnics and outdoor eating, ideal for buffets and parties and simply unbeatable for supper or lunch any day of the week.

Tagliatelle, Cottage Cheese and Pine Nut Salad

SERVES 4	METRIC	IMPERIAL	AMERICAN
Green (spinach) tagliatelle	*225 g*	*8 oz*	*8 oz*
Olive oil	*60 ml*	*4 tbsp*	*4 tbsp*
Red (bell) pepper, chopped	*1*	*1*	*1*
Green pepper, chopped	*1*	*1*	*1*
Spring onions (scallions), chopped	*4*	*4*	*4*
Pine nuts, roughly crushed	*100 g*	*4 oz*	*1 cup*
Cottage cheese	*450 g*	*1 lb*	*2 cups*
Salt and freshly ground black pepper			
Lettuce leaves, a little extra olive oil and wedges of lemon, to garnish			

1 Cook the tagliatelle according to the packet directions. Drain, rinse with cold water and drain again.

2 Add the oil and toss thoroughly.

3 Add the remaining ingredients and toss gently until well blended.

4 Pile on a bed of lettuce, drizzle with a little extra oil and garnish with lemon wedges.

PREPARATION TIME:
10 MINUTES

COOKING TIME:
12 MINUTES

TV Salad Supper

This makes a highly nutritious supper dish, ideal for eating with a fork while watching television!

SERVES 4	METRIC	IMPERIAL	AMERICAN
Ruote	*225 g*	*8 oz*	*8 oz*
Tomatoes, chopped	*4*	*4*	*4*
Cucumber, diced	*¼*	*¼*	*¼*
Cheddar cheese, cubed	*175 g*	*6 oz*	*6 oz*
Can of sweetcorn (corn), drained	*320 g*	*12 oz*	*1 large*
Olive oil	*45 ml*	*3 tbsp*	*3 tbsp*
Lemon juice	*15 ml*	*1 tbsp*	*1 tbsp*
Dijon mustard	*5 ml*	*1 tsp*	*1 tsp*
Salt	*1.5 ml*	*¼ tsp*	*¼ tsp*
Freshly ground black pepper			
Little gem lettuce, cut into pieces	*1*	*1*	*1*

1 Cook the ruote according to the packet directions. Drain, rinse with cold water and drain again.

2 Put the ruote, tomatoes, cucumber and cheese in a bowl with the sweetcorn and mix gently.

3 Whisk the remaining ingredients except the lettuce together and pour over. Toss lightly. Chill, if liked. Add the lettuce, toss again and serve in bowls.

PREPARATION TIME:
8 MINUTES

COOKING TIME:
10 MINUTES

Mozzarella and Cherry Tomato Conchiglie

Clean-tasting and refreshing – one of the most delicious summer lunch dishes imaginable.

SERVES 4	METRIC	IMPERIAL	AMERICAN
Conchiglie	*225 g*	*8 oz*	*8 oz*
Mozzarella cheese, cut into small dice	*225 g*	*8 oz*	*8 oz*
Cherry tomatoes, quartered	*350 g*	*12 oz*	*12 oz*
Basil leaves, torn	*16*	*16*	*16*
Olive oil	*250 ml*	*8 fl oz*	*1 cup*
Red wine vinegar	*30 ml*	*2 tbsp*	*2 tbsp*
Freshly ground black pepper			
Lollo rosso lettuce and a little coarse sea salt, to garnish			

1 Cook the conchiglie. Drain, rinse with cold water. Drain again and place in a large bowl.

2 Add all the remaining ingredients, including lots of black pepper. Toss lightly and chill for 30 minutes.

3 Line a salad bowl with lollo rosso leaves. Pile the salad in the centre and serve sprinkled with a little coarse sea salt.

PREPARATION TIME:
8 MINUTES
PLUS CHILLING TIME

COOKING TIME:
10 MINUTES

Curried Chicken Mayonnaise

This is also delicious tossed into cold cooked rice. For more spice, increase the amount of curry paste used, or add a pinch of chilli powder.

SERVES 4	METRIC	IMPERIAL	AMERICAN
Wholewheat penne	*225 g*	*8 oz*	*8 oz*
Mayonnaise	*60 ml*	*4 tbsp*	*4 tbsp*
Mango chutney	*30 ml*	*2 tbsp*	*2 tbsp*
Curry paste	*10 ml*	*2 tsp*	*2 tsp*
Cooked chicken, roughly chopped	*175 g*	*6 oz*	*1½ cups*

Mixed salad leaves, paprika and lemon wedges, to garnish

1 Cook the penne according to the packet directions. Drain, rinse with cold water and drain again.

2 Blend the mayonnaise in a bowl with the mango chutney and curry paste.

3 Fold in the cooked chicken and pasta and chill until ready to serve.

4 Pile on to a bed of mixed salad leaves. Garnish with paprika and lemon wedges before serving.

PREPARATION TIME:
5 MINUTES
PLUS CHILLING TIME

COOKING TIME:
15 MINUTES

Provence-style Salad

SERVES 4

Rigatoni	*225 g*	*8 oz*	*8 oz*
French (green) beans, cut into thirds	*225 g*	*8 oz*	*8 oz*
Hard-boiled (hard-cooked) eggs, roughly chopped	*2*	*2*	*2*
Small onion, sliced and separated into rings	*1*	*1*	*1*
Tomatoes, diced	*4*	*4*	*4*
Can of tuna, drained	*185 g*	*6½ oz*	*1 small*
Can of anchovies, drained and cut into thin slivers	*50 g*	*2 oz*	*1 small*
Olive oil	*90 ml*	*6 tbsp*	*6 tbsp*
Red wine vinegar	*30 ml*	*2 tbsp*	*2 tbsp*
Salt and freshly ground black pepper			
Cos (romaine) lettuce	*¼*	*¼*	*¼*
Chopped parsley and a few black olives, to garnish			

1 Cook the rigatoni in boiling salted water for 5 minutes, then add the beans and cook for a further 5 minutes until just tender. Drain, rinse with cold water and drain again.

2 Place in a bowl with the remaining ingredients and season lightly with salt and add lots of black pepper. Toss very gently. Garnish with parsley and olives.

PREPARATION TIME: 10 MINUTES

COOKING TIME: 10 MINUTES

Warm Crunchy Fried Bread and Herb Tagliatelle Salad

SERVES 4	METRIC	IMPERIAL	AMERICAN
Fresh tagliatelle, bought or home-made (see page 156)	*450 g*	*1 lb*	*1 lb*
Wholemeal breadcrumbs	*225 g*	*8 oz*	*4 cups*
Tomatoes, chopped	*12*	*12*	*12*
Sprigs of thyme, chopped	*4*	*4*	*4*
Chopped basil	*45 ml*	*3 tbsp*	*3 tbsp*
Chopped parsley	*45 ml*	*3 tbsp*	*3 tbsp*
Salt and freshly ground black pepper			
Olive oil	*120 ml*	*4 fl oz*	*½ cup*
Garlic cloves, crushed	*3*	*3*	*3*
Lettuce leaves and freshly grated Parmesan cheese, to serve			

1 Cook the pasta for 4 minutes in boiling, salted water. Drain and leave to cool slightly.

2 Dry-fry (sauté) the breadcrumbs in a large frying pan (skillet), tossing all the time until crisp but not browned.

3 Mix the tomatoes with the herbs, salt and lots of pepper in a bowl with the tagliatelle.

4 Heat the oil in a frying pan, add the breadcrumbs and garlic and fry (sauté) until golden brown. Add to the bowl and toss well.

5 Pile into bowls lined with lettuce leaves. Dust with Parmesan and serve warm.

PREPARATION TIME: 5 MINUTES

COOKING TIME: 10 MINUTES

Spiced Avocado Salad

SERVES 4	METRIC	IMPERIAL	AMERICAN
Green (spinach) fettuccini	*350 g*	*12 oz*	*12 oz*
Ripe avocados, peeled and stoned (pitted)	*2*	*2*	*2*
Lemon juice	*30 ml*	*2 tbsp*	*2 tbsp*
Worcestershire sauce	*30 ml*	*2 tbsp*	*2 tbsp*
Grated onion	*5 ml*	*1 tsp*	*1 tsp*
Chilli powder	*2.5 ml*	*½ tsp*	*½ tsp*
Olive oil	*60 ml*	*4 tbsp*	*4 tbsp*
Salt and freshly ground black pepper			
Piece of cucumber, finely diced	*5 cm*	*2 in*	*2 in*
Tomatoes, seeded and chopped	*2*	*2*	*2*
Red (bell) pepper, diced	*½*	*½*	*½*
A little extra olive oil and crushed tortilla chips, to garnish			

1 Cook the pasta according to the packet directions. Drain, rinse with cold water and drain again.

2 Dice the avocados and toss with the lemon juice.

3 Whisk the Worcestershire sauce, the onion and the chilli powder with the oil until blended. Season to taste with salt and lots of pepper.

4 Add the pasta, cucumber, tomatoes and pepper to the avocado. Toss in the dressing. Chill for up to 1 hour.

5 Pile into bowls, drizzle with extra olive oil and sprinkle with crushed tortilla chips.

PREPARATION TIME:
5 MINUTES
PLUS CHILLING TIME

COOKING TIME:
10 MINUTES

Prawn Cocktail Pasta

Yes, this good old favourite is exquisite added to pasta for a main course – it makes the shellfish go further too!

SERVES 4	METRIC	IMPERIAL	AMERICAN
Farfalle	*225 g*	*8 oz*	*8 oz*
Mayonnaise	*150 ml*	*¼ pt*	*⅔ cup*
Tomato ketchup (catsup)	*15 ml*	*1 tbsp*	*1 tbsp*
Single (light) cream	*15 ml*	*1 tbsp*	*1 tbsp*
Horseradish cream	*10 ml*	*2 tsp*	*2 tsp*
Stuffed olives, chopped	*6*	*6*	*6*
Hard-boiled (hard-cooked) egg, finely chopped	*1*	*1*	*1*
Green (bell) pepper, finely chopped	*½*	*½*	*½*
Peeled prawns (shrimp)	*175 g*	*6 oz*	*1½ cups*
Shredded lettuce, snipped chives and twists of lemon, to garnish			

1 Cook the farfalle according to the packet directions. Drain, rinse with cold water and drain again.

2 Mix the mayonnaise with the tomato ketchup, cream and horseradish in a large bowl.

3 Add the pasta and the remaining ingredients and toss well but lightly. Chill until ready to serve.

4 Pile on to a bed of shredded lettuce, sprinkle with snipped chives and garnish with twists of lemon.

PREPARATION TIME:
8 MINUTES
PLUS CHILLING TIME

COOKING TIME:
10 MINUTES

OILS, BUTTERS AND PASTES

The butters and pastes are usually added to hot cooked pasta; they are then tossed to allow the delicious flavours to coat every piece or strand of the pasta and served straight away. All the pastes can be made in advance and stored in a screw-topped jar in the fridge for up to a week. Each is enough for 350–450 g/12 oz–1 lb pasta. Try adding a spoonful of any of the pastes to soups or casseroles for a stunning Mediterranean flavour. You'll also find a very simple recipe for fresh pasta in this chapter for those of you who want to try your hand at it!

Black Butter

This simple sauce has a wonderfully nutty flavour. It is good served with any stuffed pasta and excellent with white fish too.

SERVES 4–6	METRIC	IMPERIAL	AMERICAN
Unsalted (sweet) butter	*175 g*	*6 oz*	*¾ cup*
Garlic cloves, finely chopped	*3*	*3*	*3*
Parmesan cheese, freshly grated	*175 g*	*6 oz*	*1½ cups*
Salt and freshly ground black pepper			
Chopped parsley, to garnish (optional)			

1 Put the butter in a frying pan (skillet) and melt over a moderate heat.

2 When the butter starts to foam, add the garlic and continue cooking until the butter begins to turn brown – about 1 minute. Immediately remove it from the heat – do not overcook or it will burn.

3 Stir in the Parmesan, a little salt and lots of black pepper. Add the parsley, if using. Either use at once or cool and store in the fridge until required.

PREPARATION TIME:
3 MINUTES

COOKING TIME;
3 MINUTES

Tarragon and Garlic Butter

This mixture is also good spread on slices of French bread, re-shaped into a loaf, wrapped in foil and baked in a moderate oven for 15–20 minutes.

SERVES 4	METRIC	IMPERIAL	AMERICAN
Butter, softened	*100 g*	*4 oz*	*½ cup*
Chopped tarragon	*30 ml*	*2 tbsp*	*2 tbsp*
Garlic cloves, crushed	*2*	*2*	*2*
Freshly ground black pepper			

1 Mash the butter with the tarragon, garlic and a good grinding of pepper until well blended.

2 Shape into a roll on a sheet of greaseproof (waxed) paper or clingfilm (plastic wrap). Roll up and chill until required.

3 Cut into slices or pieces before adding to pasta.

PREPARATION TIME:
5 MINUTES

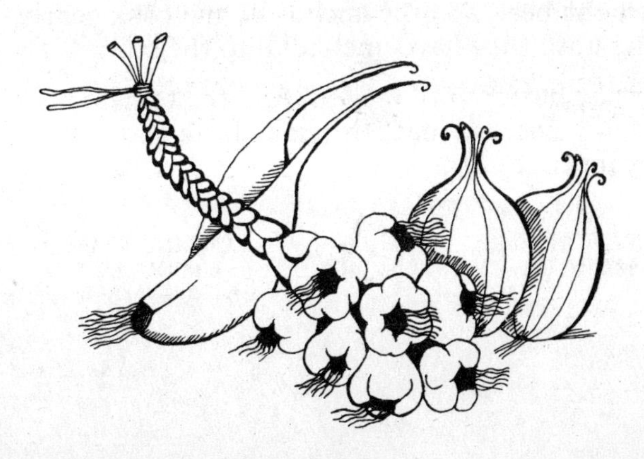

Bagna Cauda

This delicious concoction comes from the Piedmont region of Italy. Sometimes it is flavoured with white truffles, sometimes with walnut oil. It is often served like a fondue in the middle of the table with a selection of vegetables to dip in. It also makes a sensational dressing for pasta.

SERVES 4–6	METRIC	IMPERIAL	AMERICAN
Walnut oil	*75 ml*	*5 tbsp*	*5 tbsp*
Olive oil	*75 ml*	*5 tbsp*	*5 tbsp*
Garlic cloves, finely chopped	*3*	*3*	*3*
Can of anchovy fillets, drained and chopped	*50 g*	*2 oz*	*1 small*
Unsalted (sweet) butter	*25 g*	*1 oz*	*2 tbsp*
Tomato, seeded and chopped	*1*	*1*	*1*
Double (heavy) cream (optional)	*45 ml*	*3 tbsp*	*3 tbsp*
Freshly ground black pepper			

1 Heat the oil in a saucepan. Add the garlic and fry (sauté) until golden.

2 Reduce the heat, add the anchovies and cook gently, stirring until they have 'melted' into the oil.

3 Stir in the butter until melted. Add the tomato and cream, if using, and heat through. Taste and add a little pepper, if liked.

PREPARATION TIME:
5 MINUTES

COOKING TIME:
6 MINUTES

Aglio e Olio

Fresh root ginger is a popular flavouring in Umbria, central Italy. This flavoured oil can be either used straight away or poured into a screw-topped jar and kept for up to 3 weeks in the fridge. Reheat before pouring over pasta.

SERVES 4–6	METRIC	IMPERIAL	AMERICAN
Olive oil	*375 ml*	*13 fl oz*	*1½ cups*
Garlic cloves, chopped	*10*	*10*	*10*
Grated fresh root ginger	*45 ml*	*3 tbsp*	*3 tbsp*

1 Heat the oil in a saucepan. Add the garlic and ginger and cook for 2–3 minutes until lightly golden.

2 Remove from the heat and either use straight away or cool slightly and store as above.

PREPARATION TIME:
5 MINUTES

COOKING TIME:
4 MINUTES

Pesto alla Genovese

This classic paste is one of the highlights of Italian pasta cooking. Don't be tempted to try and use dried basil – it simply won't work.

SERVES 4	METRIC	IMPERIAL	AMERICAN
Large basil leaves	*20*	*20*	*20*
Garlic cloves, crushed	*2*	*2*	*2*
Coarse sea salt	*5 ml*	*1 tsp*	*1 tsp*
Pine nuts	*30 ml*	*2 tbsp*	*2 tbsp*
Freshly grated Parmesan cheese	*30 ml*	*2 tbsp*	*2 tbsp*
Olive oil	*60 ml*	*4 tbsp*	*4 tbsp*
Freshly ground black pepper			

1 Place the basil leaves in a blender or food processor with the garlic and salt and run the machine until they form a purée. Alternatively, you can pound the ingredients in a pestle and mortar.

2 Add the nuts and cheese and blend until smooth, scraping the mixture from the sides as necessary.

3 Gradually add the oil, a drop at a time, until the mixture becomes a thick, green sauce. Add a good grinding of pepper.

PREPARATION TIME:
8–10 MINUTES

Almond and Herb Paste

This is an anglicised version of Pesto alla Genovese, but it has an equally fragrant aroma and tempting flavour.

SERVES 4	METRIC	IMPERIAL	AMERICAN
Butter	*100 g*	*4 oz*	*½ cup*
Ground almonds	*50 g*	*2 oz*	*½ cup*
Freshly grated Parmesan cheese	*20 ml*	*4 tsp*	*4 tsp*
Chopped parsley	*45 ml*	*3 tbsp*	*3 tbsp*
Snipped chives	*15 ml*	*1 tbsp*	*1 tbsp*
Chopped sage	*10 ml*	*2 tsp*	*2 tsp*
Salt and freshly ground black pepper			

1 Mash the butter with the ground almonds.

2 Work in the cheese and herbs and season well.

PREPARATION TIME:
8 MINUTES

Spinach and Cashew Nut Paste

Another gloriously green paste but with a more subtle flavour than Pesto.

SERVES 4–6	METRIC	IMPERIAL	AMERICAN
Young spinach leaves	*350 g*	*12 oz*	*12 oz*
Grated Pecorino cheese	*100 g*	*4 oz*	*1 cup*
Shelled cashew nuts	*100 g*	*4 oz*	*1 cup*
Garlic cloves, crushed	*2*	*2*	*2*
Lemon juice	*30 ml*	*2 tbsp*	*2 tbsp*
Olive oil	*250 ml*	*8 fl oz*	*1 cup*
Salt and freshly ground black pepper			

1 Chop the spinach in a blender or food processor.

2 Add the cheese, nuts, garlic and lemon juice and run the machine until well blended.

3 Add the olive oil in a thin stream, with the machine running all the time, until a smooth paste is formed.

4 Season lightly with salt and pepper. If the sauce is too thick, add a little hot water.

PREPARATION TIME:
5 MINUTES

Sun-dried Tomato Paste

Sun-dried tomatoes in olive oil are now readily available in most supermarkets. They are often found along with other Italian antipastos. For an alternative version, omit the nuts and parsley and add 8 basil leaves.

SERVES 4–6	METRIC	IMPERIAL	AMERICAN
Jar of sun-dried tomatoes, drained, reserving the oil	*285 g*	*10½ oz*	*1 small*
Olive oil			
Parmesan cheese, freshly grated	*150 g*	*5 oz*	*1¼ cups*
Chopped mixed nuts	*75 g*	*3 oz*	*¾ cup*
Chopped parsley	*45 ml*	*3 tbsp*	*3 tbsp*
Garlic cloves	*3*	*3*	*3*

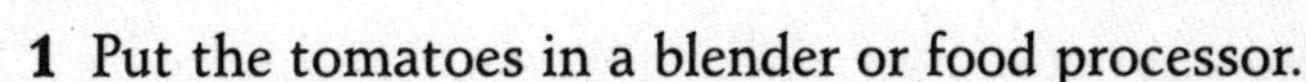

1. Put the tomatoes in a blender or food processor.
2. Make up the reserved tomato oil to 325 ml/11 fl oz/ 1½ cups with olive oil.
3. Add the oil to the blender with the remaining ingredients. Run the machine until the mixture forms a smooth paste, stopping the machine and scraping down the sides from time to time.
4. If the paste is too thick, add a little hot water.

PREPARATION TIME:
5 MINUTES

Pimiento and Olive Paste

Made mainly from storecupboard ingredients, this paste is ideal for an impromptu supper party. A good tip is to keep a bag of parsley in the freezer. The flavour is just as good as when the leaves are fresh.

SERVES 4–6	METRIC	IMPERIAL	AMERICAN
Can of pimientos, drained	*400 g*	*14 oz*	*1 large*
Garlic cloves	*2*	*2*	*2*
Olive oil	*300 ml*	*½ pt*	*1¼ cups*
Stuffed olives	*75 g*	*3 oz*	*½ cup*
Parmesan cheese, freshly grated	*50 g*	*2 oz*	*½ cup*
Chopped parsley	*60 ml*	*4 tbsp*	*4 tbsp*
Lemon juice	*30 ml*	*2 tbsp*	*2 tbsp*
Salt and freshly ground black pepper			

1 Put all the ingredients except the salt and pepper into a food processor or blender.

2 Run the machine until the mixture forms a paste. Stop the machine and scrape down the sides from time to time.

3 Taste and season with a little salt and lots of black pepper.

PREPARATION TIME:
5 MINUTES

Tapenade

This is a famous paste from Provence. It is delicious as a pasta dressing or spread on slices of crusty French bread.

SERVES 4–6	METRIC	IMPERIAL	AMERICAN
Olive oil	*250 ml*	*8 fl oz*	*1 cup*
Black olives, stoned (pitted)	*225 g*	*8 oz*	*1⅓ cups*
Green olives, stoned	*225 g*	*8 oz*	*1⅓ cups*
Garlic cloves	*3*	*3*	*3*
Parsley	*75 g*	*3 oz*	*3 oz*
Cans of anchovies, drained	*2×50 g*	*2×2 oz*	*2 small*
Capers, drained	*60 ml*	*4 tbsp*	*4 tbsp*
Lemon juice	*45 ml*	*3 tbsp*	*3 tbsp*
Freshly ground black pepper			

1 Put all the ingredients in a food processor or blender.

2 Run the machine until a smooth paste is formed. Stop the machine and scrape down the sides from time to time.

PREPARATION TIME:
6 MINUTES

Quick and Easy Fresh Pasta

You can mix the dough by hand, working the flour into the eggs and then kneading until smooth, but it takes longer!

SERVES 4	METRIC	IMPERIAL	AMERICAN
Eggs	*3*	*3*	*3*
Strong (bread) flour	*275 g*	*10 oz*	*2½ cups*
Flour for dusting			
Salt			
Olive oil	*15 ml*	*1 tbsp*	*1 tbsp*

1 Break the eggs into a food processor and run the machine for 30 seconds.

2 Add the flour and blend for a further 30 seconds or until the mixture forms a soft but not sticky dough.

3 Turn out on to a floured board and knead until the dough is smooth and elastic, adding a little more flour if getting sticky.

4 Wrap in a polythene bag and leave on the side for 30 minutes to rest.

5 On a large floured work surface, roll out and stretch the dough, rolling away from you and giving it a quarter turn every so often until it is almost thin enough to see through and hanging over the edge of the work surface. For shapes, cut now (see page 157); for tagliatelle, cover with a cloth and leave for 15 minutes before cutting.

Cannelloni/Lasagne
Cut the rolled-out dough into oblongs 10×13 cm/ 4×5 in. Boil in lightly salted water for 1 minute, then place in a bowl of cold water with 5 ml/1 tsp oil added. Drain on a damp cloth.

Farfalle
Cut the rolled-out dough into 5 cm/2 in squares with a fluted pastry wheel. Pinch the squares diagonally across the middle to form butterflies or bows.

Maltagliate
This literally means 'badly cut'. Simply cut the rolled-out dough into small triangles about the size of a thumb nail. Used mainly in soups.

Pappardelle
Cut the rolled-out dough with a plain or fluted cutter into strips 2 cm/¾ in wide.

Tagliatelle
Roll up the rested sheet of pasta like a Swiss (jelly) roll. Cut into slices about 5 mm/¼ in thick. Unroll and drape over a clean cloth on the back of a chair (or a clothes-horse) while you cut the rest.

To Cook
Allow 100 g/4 oz/1 cup fresh pasta per person.

1 Bring a large pan of lightly salted water to the boil.

2 Add 15 ml/1 tbsp olive oil or a knob of butter and the pasta and cook for about 4 minutes until almost tender but not soggy (*al dente*). Drain and use as required.

INDEX

aglio e olio 149
almond and herb paste 151
anchovies
  bagna cauda 148
  green goddess 114–15
  tagliatelle alla rustica 71
  tapenade 155
artichokes, caviare and prawns 61
asparagus, pappardelle with green hollandaise 104–5
aubergines
  golden pepper with aubergine tagliatelle 94–5
  rustic aubergines with red kidney beans 92–3
avocados
  fresh Parmesan with avocado tortellini 127
  spiced avocado salad 143

bacon
  cannelloni ripieni 24–5
  chanterelle cream ragu 99
  pasta all'Amatriciana 25
  Sardinian clams with bacon 54
  scallop and bacon wheels 69
  spaghetti alla carbonara 133
  spaghetti Napoletana 31
  TV supper 35
bagna cauda 148
beef
  beef Stroganoff 20–1
  bucatini with steak sauce 18–19
  family spaghetti Bolognese 14
  lasagne al forno 17
  simple meat lasagne 15
  spaghetti with meatballs 22–3
  tagliatelle Bolognese classico 16–17
brandied crab supper 66–7
breads 12
broccoli
  Ricotta cheese and broccoli tagliatelle 120
  smoked salmon, egg and broccoli tagliatelle 73
  walnut and broccoli sensation 87
cannellini beans, Tuscan tuna and beans 55
cannelloni, fresh 157
  ripieni 24–5
capellini, fiery mussel 60
carrots, spaghetti with spiced carrot and garlic purée 112–13
cashew nuts, spinach and cashew nut paste 152
cauliflower, crunchy cauliflower with coraindег tagliatelle 108–9
caviare and artichoke prawns 61
chanterelle cream ragu 99
cheese
  cheese pasta with breadcrumb crunch 121
  cheesy leek supper 116
  Dolcelatte dream 122
  farfalle with goats' cheese, radicchio and peppercorns 125
  fresh Parmesan with avocado tortellini 127
  garlic and herb tortellini 123
  goatherd's mountain special 124
  macaroni cheese 118
  nutty Gorgonzola 126
  pasta con salsa Alfredo 132
  spaghetti alla cipriota 128–9
  tagliatelle, cottage cheese and pine nut salad 137
  tagliatelle ai quattro formaggi 129
  tocco di noci 130
  TV salad supper 138
chick pea goulash 90–1
chicken
  chicken, leek and walnut pasta 48
  chicken tetrazzini 46–7
  curried chicken mayonnaise 140
  lasagne 42–3
chilli bean bonanza 88
clams
  Sardinian clams with bacon 54
  spaghetti alle vongole 50
cod
  cod and rigatoni ragu 68
  country cod and vegetable pasta casserole 70
  lasagne di mare 52–3
  Mediterranean salt cod 64–5
courgettes

Mediterranean courgette lasagne 106–7
prawn and courgette bake 62–3
crab
brandied crab supper 66–7
quick crab creation 57
cream
creamy jalapeno pepper fettucine 131
pasta con salsa Alfredo 132
curried chicken mayonnaise 140

eggs, spaghetti alla carbonara 133

garlic and herb tortellini 123
ginger, aglio e olio 149

haddock, smoked haddock bake 74–5
ham
cured ham and pea shells 30
mafalde con salsa alla panna 134
Parma ham and mushroom penne 27
tangy ham, raisin and pine nut bucatini 34–5
herbs
almond and herb paste 151
warm crunchy fried bread and herb tagliatelle salad 142

kidney beans
chilli bean bonanza 88
rustic aubergines with red kidney beans 92–3
kidney and mustard tagliarini 41

lamb
family spaghetti Bolognese 14
lamb goulash bake 38–9
pappardelle paprikash 36–7
simple meat lasagne 15
spaghetti with meatballs 22–3
lasagne
al forno 17
chicken 42–3
di mare 52–3
fresh 157
Mediterranean courgette lasagne 106–7
mushroom 96–7
simple meat lasagne 15
leeks
cheesy leek supper 116
chicken, leek and walnut pasta 48

lentils, piquant red lentil and tomato pot 83
liver, piquant chicken liver vermicelli 40

Mozzarella
and cherry tomato conchiglie 139
-topped veal and pork rigatoni 26
mushrooms
chanterelle cream ragu 99
devilled mushroom supper 98
lasagne 96–7
macaroni and mushroom cheese 119
Parma ham and mushroom penne 27
spaghetti di Napoli 84–5
spaghetti with Italian mushrooms 89
mussels
fiery mussel capellini 60
mussel magic 59

nutty Gorgonzola 126

oils, butters and pastes 145–5
olives
pimiento and olive paste 154
tapenade 155

Parma ham and mushroom penne 27
pasta
fresh 156–7
varieties 5–6
peas, creamy peas and pasta Crécy-style 103
peppers, golden pepper with aubergine tagliatelle 94–5
pesto alla Genovese 150
pimientos
pimiento and olive paste 154
salmon with pimientos and basil 76–7
pine nuts, tagliatelle, cottage cheese and pine nut salad 137
pork
mozzarella-topped veal and pork rigatoni 26
pappardelle paprikash 36–7
prawns
caviare and artichoke prawns 61
lasagne di mare 52–3
prawn cocktail pasta 144
prawn and courgette bake 62–3
Provence-style salad 141

ratatouille ruote 100–1
ravioli, spinach and ricotta 80–1
Ricotta
  Ricotta cheese and broccoli
    tagliatelle 120
  spinach and ricotta ravioli 80–1

salads 12
salmon
  with pimientos and basil 76–7
  scrambled egg and smoked salmon
    mafalde 135
  smoked salmon, egg and broccoli
    tagliatelle 73
sausages
  Italian supper 32–3
  macaroni with smoked pork
    sausage and greens 28–9
scallop and bacon wheels 69
scrambled egg and smoked salmon
  mafalde 135
seafood and fennel farfalle 51
smoked haddock bake 74–5
smoked salmon, egg and broccoli
  tagliatelle 73
spinach
  green goddess 114–15
  macaroni and spinach cheese 119
  spinach and cashew nut paste 152
  spinach and ricotta ravioli 80–1
spring greens, macaroni with
  smoked pork sausage and
    greens 28–9
squid, Roman squid and radicchio 72
store-cupboard foods 7–10
sun-dried tomato paste 153
sweetcorn
  cheesy tuna and sweetcorn grill 58
  macaroni and sweetcorn cheese 119
  quick creamy corn and vegetable
    pasta 102
  TV salad supper 138
tapenade 155
tarragon and garlic butter 147
tocca di noci 130
tomatoes
  cannelloni ripieni 24–5
  macaroni and tomato cheese
  Mozzarella and cherry tomato
    conchiglie 139
  piquant red lentil and tomato pot 83
  spaghetti di Napoli 84–5
  sun-dried tomato paste 153
  tagliatelle alla salsa di
    pomodoro 110
  tuna with tomatoes Vesuvius 56–7
  tuono e lampo 86–7
  warm crunchy fried bread and
    herb tagliatelle salad 142
tortellini
  fresh Parmesan with avocado
    tortellini 127
  garlic and herb tortellini 123
tuna
  cheesy tuna and sweetcorn grill 58
  macaroni and tuna cheese 119
  Provence-style salad 141
  with tomatoes Vesuvius 56–7
  Tuscan tuna and beans 55
tuono e lampo 86–7
turkey Veronica 44–5

veal, mozzarella-topped veal and
  pork rigatoni 26
vegetables
  country cod and vegetable pasta
    casserole 70
  quick creamy corn and vegetable
    pasta 102
  ratatouille ruote 100–1
  roast vegetable fettucci 111
  spaghettini rosmarino 82
  tagliarini primavera 79

walnut and broccoli sensation 87
walnuts, tocco di noci 130